BEFORE YOU SIGN THAT LEASE...

The Small Business Owner's Guide to Leasing Commercial Space

by

Raphael Enrique Collazo

BEFORE YOU SIGN THAT LEASE…
The Small Business Owner's Guide to Leasing Commercial Space

Copyright © 2020 by Raphael Enrique Collazo

All rights reserved.
No part of this book may be reproduced or transmitted without written permission from the author.

ISBN 978-0-9993348-7-4

Printed in the USA by Amazon KDP

DOWNLOAD THE GUIDE TO FINDING THE BEST COMMERCIAL DEALS FOR FREE!!

READ THIS FIRST:

As a thank you for buying my book, I'd like to give you the customized guide to finding the best commercial deals I created

100% FREE!

TO DOWNLOAD, GO TO:
https://bit.ly/2Q0y4MW

FOLLOW ME ON SOCIAL MEDIA!

YouTube: https://bit.ly/2ZtLV3j
Facebook: https://bit.ly/2Ya9Ork
Instagram: @commercial_louisville

DEDICATION

There are so many people to thank for the completion of this book. The writing process is a team effort and without such a stellar one in my corner, I would have never reached the finish line.

First, I want to thank my family for constantly supporting me and my work. You have showed me what it means to live an honorable life and I'll be forever grateful to you.

Second, I'd like to thank my beautiful, smart and confident girlfriend Melanie. Since we've met, you have been my biggest cheerleader. I love you with all my heart and I can't wait for what our future holds.

Finally, I'm proud to dedicate this book to the entrepreneurs who make our economy turn. Without your dedication, passion, and willingness to take risks, the *"American Dream"* as we know it would cease to exist.

All the best,

Raphael Collazo

TABLE OF CONTENTS

Dedication		5
Introduction		9
Chapter 1	Beginning Your Journey	13
Chapter 2	Determining Your Needs	21
Chapter 3	Setting Expectations	29
Chapter 4	Assembling Your Real Estate Advisory Team	35
Chapter 5	Understanding Commercial Leases	45
Chapter 6	Calculating Your Monthly Cash Outflow	53
Chapter 7	Securing Your New Space	61
Chapter 8	Negotiating Lease Terms	67
Chapter 9	Completing Your Build-Out	81
Chapter 10	Tying Up Loose Ends	93
Chapter 11	Implementing A Marketing Strategy	99
Chapter 12	Opening Your Doors!	109
Bio		115
Book Recommendations		117
Real Estate Terminology		121
References		135

INTRODUCTION

Welcome to the wonderful world of commercial real estate! It's an exciting industry and one that's an important part of the entrepreneurial journey. Since becoming a commercial real estate agent in 2019, I've had the privilege of helping many business owners turn their dreams into a reality. However, as I worked with my clients to help them lease commercial space, I realized just how little was known about the process. There are plenty of resources available for those interested in buying and/or renting residential real estate. However, that's not the case for commercial real estate. In fact, many of the resources out there are intentionally vague and difficult to comprehend.

This is particularly troubling because business owners already have the deck stacked against them. The reality is, 50% of businesses fail within the first 5 years of opening their doors. The primary reason for this is that they run out of cash. My goal with this book is to significantly reduce that number by helping entrepreneurs make better decisions regarding one of their biggest line items; their rent/mortgage payment. In this book, I have laid out a 12-step program that will help you get from idea to opening your doors as quickly and seamlessly as possible. The insights contained in this book include:

1) **Beginning your journey** – We will review the pros and cons of leasing commercial property and determine if it's the right move for you and your business.
2) **Determining your needs** – We will get clear on your search criteria to ensure you're able to find a property that aligns with your business goals.
3) **Setting Expectations** – I will share insights on what to expect throughout the leasing process and explain the items you should prepare prior to beginning your search.
4) **Assembling your real estate advisory team** – We will learn how to recruit an all-star real estate team that will help you secure the best property for your business needs as well as protect your best interests.
5) **Understanding commercial lease types** – We will learn about the different commercial lease types and determine which one is appropriate given your business use.
6) **Calculating your monthly cash outflow** – We will explain how to properly calculate your monthly cash outflow to ensure you are able to fulfill your financial obligations.
7) **Securing your space** – We will walk through how to draft and submit your lease proposal to a landlord.
8) **Negotiating lease terms** – We will learn about a host of potential lease provisions and share strategies on how to effectively negotiate favorable lease terms.

9) **Completing your build out** – *If your space needs to be renovated, we will explain how to solicit the services of a competent and competitively priced commercial contractor as well as how to effectively manage the project to its completion.*

10) **Tying up loose ends** – *We will highlight various items you need to address prior to occupying your space.*

11) **Implementing a marketing strategy** – *We will learn about some of the most effective marketing strategies and how you can use them to grow your business over time.*

12) **Opening your doors** – *You have finally made it to the finish line! In this section, we will explain how to create the proper systems to meet your real estate obligations and set yourself up for future expansion.*

Through it all, you will gain the knowledge and skills necessary to effectively navigate the pitfalls so many entrepreneurs face prior to opening their doors. Are you ready to take the next step towards your making your entrepreneurial dream a reality? If so, let's begin.

CHAPTER 1
BEGINNING YOUR JOURNEY

"The journey of 1000 miles begins with a single step." —**Lao Tzu**

Congratulations on making the decision to start your business! It's no small feat and I want to be the first to commend you on your passion and resolve. The purpose of this book is to outline a framework you can use to lease commercial property within the next 120 days. However, before taking the plunge, it's important to address a few items on the front end. In this chapter, we will determine if signing a commercial lease at this time is the right decision for you and your business as well as explain the pros and cons of leasing commercial space.

Do you actually need a new space?

This is the first question I ask my clients when I start working with them. Throughout my career, I've seen business owners jump the gun when signing a commercial lease. Some were tired of working from home and decided to lease office space closer to downtown. Others were aspiring restaurateurs who wanted to locate themselves in a desirable retail area. Others were small manufacturers or industrial companies who secured a space they could *"grow into"*. However, in each of these instances, they failed to understand the ramifications that come along with entering into a commercial lease agreement.

When you sign your name on the dotted line, you're committing to paying rent and possibly additional costs (i.e. taxes, insurance, maintenance etc.) for an extended period. Often, lease terms are 3 years or more! If you don't have the revenue to justify that kind of financial commitment, you could put undue strain on your business which could lead to you closing up shop completely. If you're just starting out, it may be wise to consider building up your business prior to making a long-term commitment on a space.

Not only that, but depending on your business model, it may not make much sense to secure a space at all. If you're a software developer, your business doesn't necessarily need to be tied to one geographic location. You can operate anywhere there's an internet connection. If you're a yoga instructor, you can elect to travel to your clients, thus, eliminating the overhead of having a physical location. Even if you're an aspiring restaurateur, renting a food truck can allow you to test different food combinations and travel to many locations around town to see which one is right for you.

Prior to beginning your search, I recommend working with your accountant and commercial real estate agent to create a *"personal financial statement"*. This document will lay out your total cash flows as well as your assets and liabilities. To download a copy of the one I provide to my clients, check out my resources page at www.raphaelcollazo.com/resources. If you don't have enough cashflow to justify at least $1,000 per month in building related expenses, you may not be ready to commit to leasing commercial space. Remember, there's nothing wrong with waiting until you're in a stronger financial position to justify expanding. By limiting your overhead, you can allocate more resources toward growing your business so that once you turn the corner, it will be healthy enough to take on the financial commitment.

> **Pro- tip:** If you're currently a one-person operation, consider outsourcing work to expand your capacity to take on new clients. For example, if you're a graphic designer who helps businesses create and market their brand, hiring contractors to take on the design activities can free you up to perform your business's most important functions; securing new business and interacting with your existing clients. There are plenty of qualified professionals on sites like www.upwork.com and www.fiverr.com who produce high quality work at competitive prices.

The pros and cons of commercial leasing

Now that you've determined that you're able to take on the financial responsibility of leasing commercial space, it's important to educate yourself on the commercial leasing process. Below I've outlined the pros and cons of leasing commercial space and provided feedback on when it's best to pursue it as your primary option:

Pros:

1) **Low initial investment** – Unlike purchasing a commercial property, signing a lease does not require a large down payment. In most cases, all you are required to pay initially is your first month's rent and a security deposit. This significantly reduces your up-front costs and allows you to use more of your capital to operate your business.

2) **Flexibility** – Leasing a commercial property can afford you more flexibility. For example, in the Louisville market, tenants usually sign a lease for a short period of time (3-5 years). After their term expires, they are free to either leave or negotiate new terms with the landlord. If you're someone who values the freedom to move if necessary, signing a lease with a fixed term affords you that opportunity.

3) **Negotiable terms** – Where banks tend to be more rigid and procedural, landlords are usually more creative. They don't often conduct a strict multivariant analysis to determine whether you're eligible to occupy space in their building. If you're a reputable individual with a

solid financial standing and you're willing to sign a 3-5-year lease, your commercial real estate agent should be able to negotiate favorable lease terms for you.

Cons:

1) **Lack of control** – One of the biggest down-sides of leasing commercial space is the lack of control. Depending on the economic environment, you may have little to no leverage when negotiating with a landlord on your rental rate and other expenses. Along with that, when your lease term ends, the landlord may decide to raise rents or not continue renting the space to you. This can be a huge setback for your business if you've already established yourself in the area.

2) **No equity** – When you lease a commercial property, you don't get to capitalize on the benefit of building equity. If you lease a space for 5 years, you will have nothing to show for your years of making rent payments. On the other hand, if you were to purchase a building and make 5 years of mortgage payments, you will have paid off a significant portion of the loan. Not only that, you could also build equity by making improvements to the structure or just by the natural appreciation of real estate.

3) **Higher monthly rents** – In most instances, if you lease commercial space, you will make higher monthly payments than someone who owns a similar property. This is because your landlord must pay a mortgage, taxes, insurance, maintenance, and repairs costs. On top of that, they will want to make a profit on their

investment. As a result, all these items will be factored into your monthly rental payment.

Generally, if you plan on occupying a space for a long period of time, you would be wise to consider buying a property to capitalize on equity build-up and appreciation. However, if you want to maintain flexibility, limit your initial investment, and/or have more working capital available to help you get your business off the ground, leasing a commercial property may be your best approach. Since you're reading this book, I'm moving forward under the assumption that you've chosen to lease commercial space. Now that you've made your decision, let's talk about best way of doing that.

Action Items

1) Determine if your business is financially strong enough to take on the commitment of leasing commercial space.
    a. If it's not, continue expanding until you can.
2) Review the pros and cons of leasing a commercial space.
    a. Determine if leasing or buying a commercial property is right for you and your business.

CHAPTER 2
DETERMINING YOUR NEEDS

"Understanding the needs of your business is the starting point for any project."
—**John Williams**

Prior to securing a new space, you must first get clear on what your current needs are. It doesn't make sense to start looking for properties prior to knowing exactly what your business requires and what you can afford. In this section, we will seek to define the following criteria: your budget, size requirements and desired location.

Budget

This is probably the most important variable to consider prior to beginning your search. Although there's no one size fits all approach to determining how much rent you can afford, there is a method that offers business owners a good starting point. This calculation is known as your *"rent-to-revenue"* ratio.

Your rent to revenue ratio is the percentage of money your business spends on rent in relation to your business's gross income. For example, let's imagine you identify a space that rents for $2,000 per month or $24,000 per year. If your projected revenue for the year is $150,000, your rent to revenue ratio would be 16 percent ($24,000/$150,000).

Given this percentage, you may be wondering, *"Is 16% acceptable?"*. Unfortunately, the answer is *"it depends"*. If you run a law firm, a ratio of around 15 percent may be acceptable. However, if you're the owner of a low-margin business such as a restaurant, you may be safer pursuing a space where the rent to revenue ratio is between 5 to 10 percent. Although this is not an exact science, it gives you a good idea of how much rent you can afford. Below I've provided a list of average rent to revenue ratios for different types of businesses:

- **Law firms:** *Attorney offices should expect to pay 6–7% of gross revenue, and even up to 15% for a prestigious address.*
- **Restaurants:** *When calculating a good rent percentage for restaurants, the general rule of thumb is your total occupancy cost (rent and additional fees for property taxes, insurances, etc.) should not exceed 6–10% of your gross sales.*
- **Auto shops:** *The typical full-service auto shop spends 12–13% of annual gross revenues on rent.*
- **Retail stores:** *Retailers should target a base rental rate that is no more than 5–10% of gross annual sales.*

- **Hair salons:** Rent and property taxes should range from 3% for a remote location to 10% in a well-trafficked mall.

*If you don't see your business on the list, do some research and/or work with your commercial real estate agent to determine what ratio range is appropriate.

Having said that, this ratio doesn't outweigh your individual situation. If you don't have enough cash on hand to afford the first month's rent, it doesn't matter how good your ratio is. Likewise, if your income fluctuates wildly or you're unsure about your revenue projections, it may be wise to be more conservative when creating your budget. It also pays to think about what happens if things go wrong, like your biggest client suddenly deciding to jump ship. Performing this analysis ahead of time will give you a better understanding of what you can afford and will help your commercial real estate agent narrow down a list of properties that align with this reality.

> **Pro-tip:** As a rule of thumb, try to have at least 3-6 months of expenses saved up prior to beginning your search. This will provide you with enough of a financial cushion to start your occupancy off on the right foot. You can use this extra capital to weather the early months of building demand in your market, purchasing equipment (i.e. P.O.S systems, tables, chairs, racks etc.) and various other items that enable you to operate a functional establishment.

Size

The second item to consider is how much space you will need to operate your business. In commercial real estate, the metric most often used to describe this requirement is your total *"square footage"* (SF). Like your budget, size requirements will vary widely depending on your use. For example, if you run a manufacturing business, you may need to lease a large warehouse with high ceilings and plenty of open space to operate heavy machinery, store raw materials, as well as a host of other functions.

On the other hand, if you're looking to secure an office lease, your space requirement will be completely different. In this scenario, a good rule of thumb would be to factor in between 125–200 SF per person. This range accounts for a 10x12 foot office per person plus additional space for waiting rooms, walkways, reception areas etc. As a result, if you're running a 10-person operation, your space requirement will likely be anywhere between 1,250–2500 SF.

If you own a retail business, your space requirement will be dependent on what goods/services you're selling, how much inventory you need to store, how many employees you have etc. For example, grocers usually require much more open space than service businesses such as barbers, nail salons, chiropractors etc. Along with that, restaurants need to have dedicated space for a dining area as well as room for a kitchen. The space must also comply with city codes and regulations to ensure the proper and safe operation of the restaurant.

Location

You've probably heard the saying that real estate is all about *"location, location, location"*. However, the ideal location for one business owner will not be the same for another. For example, if you're a retailer, occupying a space that has great visibility along major roadways will be of value to you. As a result, you may elect to place your store along a road with high traffics counts, great visibility, and accessibility.

If you want to open an insurance office, you may not care how visible the property is. Because of this, you may opt to sign a lease for a larger space in a more remote location with ample parking. At the other end of the spectrum, if you operate a manufacturing business, being close to your primary suppliers and having easy access to major roadways will be critical. Because of this variability, you need to get clear on your business goals and define how each of these requirements will help you achieve your objectives. Some of the questions to consider include:

- *Is the property located in an area suitable for your use?*
    - *Is it near offices, homes, other businesses?*
    - *Is it close to interstates and/or roads with high traffic counts?*
- *How easy is it to drive to the property?*
    - *Is there a dedicated turn lane to enter and exit?*
    - *Can you access it from a major roadway, or do you have to turn onto a side road to do so?*

- *If you're a retailer, service professional and/or restaurateur:*
    o *Are potential customers able to see your establishment?*
    o *Is it tucked away behind other buildings and/or another major retail center?*
    o *Do you have signs on the premises you can utilize?*

Your commercial real estate agent should help you answer these questions as well as provide you with the data you'll need to make an informed decision on each property.

> **Pro-tip:** Keep your budget in mind when defining the best location for your business. If you require 2,000 SF to operate properly, a 1,000 SF space downtown won't work, regardless of how good the location is. Likewise, if your budget is $1,500 per month, you likely won't be able to afford a large penthouse office suite in your city's Central Business District (C.B.D).

Action Items

1) Determine how much you can afford to spend each month on rent and other building expenses.
2) Get clear on how much space you'll need to operate your business.
    a. Ensure it's functional for your use.
        i. Will you need storage, a commercial kitchen, bay doors etc.?
3) Analyze where the best location for your business would be.
    a. Consider why being located in that area will help your business grow.
        i. Are you giving up something of significance to be in that location?

CHAPTER 3
SETTING EXPECTATIONS

"Disappointment is the gap that exists between expectation and reality." —**John C. Maxwell**

As we highlighted in the previous chapter, the first thing I do when I begin working with a new client is to sit down with them to discuss their budget, space and location requirements as well as their business goals and aspirations. From there, I communicate the realities of the commercial leasing process and set expectations to prepare them for the road ahead. During this initial consultation, I share 3 main points that new business owners must understand prior to beginning their search for commercial space. To make your leasing experience as seamless as possible, I've shared these important points below:

There's no such thing as a *"perfect property"*

Unfortunately, I'm here to be the bearer of bad news. Regardless of your expectations, there's no such thing as the *"perfect"* property. Throughout my career, I've seen small business owners fall victim to this trap time and time again. Many have this fairytale idea of what their business will look like. From the business cards, to the banners, to the layout, to the furniture, to the location and everything in between. They believe this perfect space is out there and that they will discover it if they look hard enough. Unfortunately, it's often not the case and their lack of success can lead to them becoming disheartened with the entire process.

There will always be something about a property you wish would be different. Whether it's wanting to be located in a more desirable area, sacrificing space due to your budgetary constraints, having an odd interior layout, dealing with deferred maintenance issues etc. Unless you have unlimited resources at your disposal, these constraints, as well as many others, will arise throughout the course of your search. As a result, work with your commercial real estate agent to adjust your requirements if they don't help you achieve your ultimate objective.

Take some time this week to define your *"must have's"* and *"nice to have's"*. Your must have's are aspects of the space that contribute to the optimal operation of your business. For example, if you own an insurance company with 15 employees, you need a certain amount of space to house them. As a result, a 500 SF office is probably not going to cut it, even if it's in the best location in the world. On the other hand, if you run a manufacturing company that receives several truckloads of supplies each day, having multiple bay doors is a must. Along with that, you may require ceilings of a certain height to move materials within the facility. With my clients, I encourage them to draw a T-chart that includes all this information.

If your space doesn't look exactly the way you want it to, don't fret. As we'll learn in the *"Completing your Build Out"* chapter of the book, you can work with your general contractor to update the space to meet your unique specifications.

It usually takes longer than you think

This is one of the most common misconceptions I address on the front end of the transaction. Most new business owners don't have a frame of reference for how long it takes to secure commercial space. As a result, they often base their assumptions off their experience of buying a home. In most parts of the country, it takes no more than 60 days to purchase a residential property. Although I've helped a few of my clients secure commercial space within this timeframe, it's definitely not the norm. Usually, the process of identifying, negotiating, and occupying a new space takes many months to complete. Not only that, but if the space requires renovation, it can add several months to your timeline.

As a result, if you come into the transaction expecting a fast turnaround, you may quickly get disgruntled with the process. To avoid this from happening to you, work with your commercial real estate agent to get crystal clear on your criteria prior to beginning your search. Along with that, if your criteria are too rigid, consider modifying some of the variables to broaden your pool of potential properties. Remember, the more deals you review, the higher the likelihood you have of finding one that aligns with your business goals.

Have your financial documents in order

When you identify a space that you like, the landlord will often require you to provide financial documents to prove you and/or your business are on solid financial footing. The reason for this is that they want to ensure you're able to comply with the terms of the lease prior to allowing you to take possession of the premises. It's important to understand that landlords do not run a charity. They are investors who are seeking to make a return on their investment. As a result, they are actively searching for financially stable tenants who can prove their ability to pay rent.

Therefore, to expedite the process of securing a commercial space, make sure you have the appropriate financial documents in hand prior to beginning your search. Along with that, be willing to share them with prospective landlords when you identify a space that meets your criteria. As we'll highlight later in this book, some of these financial documents may include:

- *Personal Financial Statement*
- *Prior 3 years of Tax Returns*
- *P&L Statement*
- *Balance Sheet*
- *Credit Reports (Personal & Business)*
- *Etc.*

Although this may seem like overkill, I'm of the belief that it's better to be overly prepared than not and thus, lose an opportunity. By understanding these expectations, you will avoid a significant amount of heartache and increase the likelihood of securing a space that aligns with your business goals.

Action Items

1) *Understand that there is no such thing as a "perfect" property.*
   a. *Create a list of "must haves" and "nice to haves".*
   b. *Work with your commercial real estate agent to identify spaces that align with your list.*
2) *Understand that it usually takes longer than you think to lease commercial space.*
   a. *If your criteria are limiting your options, consider modifying them to generate more opportunities.*
3) *Work with your accountant and/or bookkeeper to compile the appropriate financial documentation prior to beginning your search.*
   a. *In the next chapter, we will identify how to find a stellar accountant who will help you accomplish this goal.*

CHAPTER 4
ASSEMBLING YOUR REAL ESTATE ADVISORY TEAM

"Alone we can do so little; together we can do so much." —**Helen Keller**

Now that you've clearly defined your requirements and understand the expectations for the leasing process, it's time to assemble your real estate advisory team. Although you're an expert in your business, you're likely not one in the area of identifying commercial property and negotiating favorable lease terms. For this reason, it's important to surround yourself with a group of stellar individuals who have a fiduciary duty to advocate for your best interests. In this section, we'll discuss how to identify and work with your real estate team to secure a property that fits your needs.

Finding a commercial real estate agent

First, you will want to solicit the services of a competent and effective commercial real estate agent. Since I am one, I'm often met with skepticism when I share this piece of advice. Probably the most common objection I hear is, *"Raphael, why should I work with a commercial real estate agent? Can't I just find a space by myself?"* Although it's not uncommon for business owners to think they can go it alone, I've seen too many suffer adverse consequences, due to their inexperience, to advocate against using one.

First, an experienced commercial real estate agent will have established relationships with owners of commercial buildings, other brokers, and reputable service professionals. They can tap into this broad network to help you identify properties that meet your criteria.

Second, they're experts in their market and can help you vet the merits of each space. They know the up and coming areas, the financial incentives offered by the city, and other location specific information that is invaluable to business owners.

Third, their familiarity with the process will help you avoid the common pitfalls that arise during commercial lease negotiations. They know the market rates, commercial lease types as well as what responsibilities should and shouldn't be passed on to the tenant.

Finally, and most importantly, they're 100% FREE for you to use! Generally, the landlord is responsible for paying the commission of the agents involved in the transaction. For this reason, you're able to capitalize on the expertise of your commercial real estate agent without incurring any cost! It's really a no-brainer.

When searching for a stellar commercial real estate agent, you'll want to make sure they have ample experience being a *"tenant representative"*. A tenant representative is an agent who focuses solely on the needs of a tenant, rather than being tied to the lessor or landlord. Here are some of the best strategies you can use to identify a potential candidate:

1) **Searching online** – Probably the easiest way to find a commercial real estate agent is to search for one online. The top agents in town are excellent marketers and will likely have several great reviews praising their ability to close difficult transactions quickly and without major issues.

2) **Asking other business owners** – Many business owners in your area will have worked with a commercial real estate agent to secure their space. If they have a positive experience with one, they will likely refer them to you.

3) **Asking your extended network** – Reach out to your network via LinkedIn, Facebook, Twitter etc. and ask them if they could recommend a commercial real estate agent. Although you'll have to sift through some self-promotional content, you'll likely get solid feedback from other business owners in your area.

4) **Calling signs** – To advertise a property for lease and/or sale, commercial real estate agents often put up signs on the premises. Like other professions, the top ones will list the most properties. If you see a lot of the same signs around town, give them a call.

Once you compile a list of potential candidates, interview each one. Some of the questions to consider asking include:

- *What geographic locations do you specialize in?*
- *How long have you been a commercial real estate agent?*
- *Can you tell me about your experience as a tenant representative?*
- *How many tenants like me have you represented?*
    - *Ask for a list of references.*
- *How will you help me analyze different spaces?*
- *Where do you see the market going?*
- *How long of a lease term should I expect?*
- *What do I need to prepare before we start the search?*
- *What else should I be asking you?*

Based on their responses, it should be evident whether theagent is a good fit for you. Finally, get clear on how you will communicate with them. Effective communication is the most important component of the real estate transaction. If you and your commercial real estate agent aren't on the same page, it will spell trouble. Therefore, if you prefer to communicate via text and email, make sure they are comfortable using those mediums. If your communication styles don't mesh, it may be wise to move on to another candidate.

> **Pro-tip:** Another common issue I see business owners face is that they decide to use residential agents to help them secure a commercial space. Although residential agents have good intentions, they're often unaware of the many moving parts involved in a commercial real estate transaction. Because of this, they often fall prey to the common obstacles inherent in the process and their clients ultimately suffer the consequences. Just like you wouldn't hire a plastic surgeon to perform a heart operation, you shouldn't ask a residential agent to handle your commercial transaction.

Finding a real estate lawyer

This is one member of your team you do not want to skimp on. A real estate lawyer is someone whose job it is to know the rules and regulations pertaining to real estate transactions. They help their clients understand real estate contracts and other legal documents. It's critical that you find an attorney who has a lot of experience working on commercial transactions. Given their expertise, they will help you avoid potentially catastrophic pitfalls that could put you at risk legally.

To find a stellar real estate attorney, start by asking your commercial real estate agent. They deal with commercial transactions daily and will likely know a few great lawyers to recommend. Along with that, ask other business owners within your network. If they're leasing commercial space and had a pleasant experience with their real estate attorney, they will likely vouch for them. Once you have a list of potential candidates, interview each one. Some of the questions to consider asking include:

- Are you primarily a real estate lawyer?
    - o If not, how much of your business is geared toward property and contract law?
- How long have you been practicing law?
- How many commercial transactions have you handled?
- How does your billing work?
- How much will your services cost?
- Will I be working with you or someone else?
    - o If someone else, how much experience do they have working in real estate law?
- Do you have references?
- What else should I be asking you?

Like your commercial real estate agent, get clear on how you will communicate with them. Effective communication is the most important component of a real estate transaction. If you and your real estate attorney aren't on the same page, it will spell trouble. Therefore, if you prefer to communicate with text and email, make sure they're comfortable using those mediums. If your communication styles don't mesh, it may be wise to move on to another candidate.

Finally, make sure they are a *"deal maker"* and not a *"deal breaker"*. What I mean by this is that some attorneys are masters at identifying problems with every action you propose. However, they don't offer any creative solutions that will help you achieve your ultimate objective while protecting your legal interests. On the other hand, stellar real estate lawyers are ones who provide alternative strategies that achieve the same or similar objectives while protecting you legally. If you plan on associating with an attorney, make sure they're the deal making kind.

Finding an accountant

These professionals are worth their weight in gold. During the leasing process, you will likely be asked to furnish various financial documents. This is because prospective landlords will want to verify that you're financially able to commit to leasing space within their building. Your accountant will work with you to compile these documents as well as ensure that the information presented is accurate. Below I've provided examples of financial documents the landlord may request:

1) ***Personal Financial Statements*** - *a disclosure of all your assets and liabilities.*

2) ***Tax Returns*** - *documents filed with a tax authority that reports your income, expenses, and other relevant financial information to assess your tax obligation.*

3) ***Profit and Loss Statements*** – *a financial document that shows the revenues and expenses of you or your company during a particular period.*

4) **Balance Sheets** – *a summary of the financial balances of you or your organization.*
5) **Credit Reports** - *a record of a borrower's responsible repayment of debts.*

Probably the best way to identify a great business accountant is by asking fellow business owners in your area. Most business owners use an accountant and will likely recommend one if they have a great working relationship. Along with that, consider asking your extended network via LinkedIn, Facebook, Twitter etc. Once you identify a few candidates, interview each one. Some of the questions to consider asking include:

- *How long have you been in business?*
- *How many businesses like me have you worked with?*
    a. *Do you have references?*
- *What services do you provide?*
- *Can you represent me in all the states I do business?*
- *Will I be working with you or someone else?*
    o *If someone else, how much experience do they have working as an accountant?*
- *Are you available year-round?*
    o *Some accounting firms shut their doors after April 15th and reopen for the following tax season.*
- *How often will we meet to discuss my business taxes?*
- *What else should I be asking you?*

Like your commercial real estate agent and real estate attorney, get clear on how you will communicate with them. If you prefer to communicate with text and email, make sure they're comfortable using those mediums as well. If your communication styles don't mesh, it may be wise to move on to another candidate. Remember, your relationship with your accountant will survive long after you lease your new commercial space. As a result, you want to make sure you select someone who's competent, responsive and has values that align with yours.

Action Items

1) Compile a list of the top commercial real estate agents in your area.
   a. Schedule an appointment to interview them and select the one that meets your criteria.
2) Ask your commercial real estate agent and your network to recommend a great real estate attorney.
   a. Once you identify a few, interview each one and select the lawyer with the best track record of success.
   b. Make sure they are a "deal maker" and not a "deal breaker".
3) Ask fellow business owners and your extended network to recommend a great accountant.
   a. Interview them and select the one who's values align with those of you and your business.
   b. Work with them to compile the financial documents you will need during your lease negotiations.

CHAPTER 5
UNDERSTANDING COMMERCIAL LEASES

"If the deal isn't good for the other party, it isn't good for you." —B.C Forbes

Now that you've assembled your all-star real estate team, it's time to learn about the different types of commercial leases. Unlike residential leases, commercial leases vary widely depending on the market, industry, comparable properties within the area etc. For that reason, it's important to properly educate yourself so you can make an informed decision based on the needs of your business. Below I've provided an overview of each:

Gross/Full-Service

This lease type is most often used in multi-tenant and single tenant office buildings, industrial and some retail properties. In a gross lease, the tenant pays a flat rent that covers all property operating expenses. These expenses may include, but are not limited to, property taxes, utilities, HVAC servicing, maintenance, trash and snow removal, parking lot clean up etc. Since the landlord is responsible for covering all these expenses, the base rental rate is typically higher than other types of leases.

Modified Gross

The second major type of commercial lease is *"modified gross"*. A modified gross (MG) lease is a type of real estate rental agreement where both the landlord and tenant are responsible for paying a property's operating expenses. These costs vary and may include property taxes, utilities, insurance, maintenance, cleaning expenses etc. The benefit of these lease agreements is that they offer a happy middle ground. Landlords can pass along some of the building's operating costs, while tenants not fully responsible for covering all property related expenses.

Having said that, who pays what in the lease agreement is 100% negotiable. It may be that both parties agree that the tenant is only responsible for covering their own utility usage. On the other hand, a landlord may negotiate an agreement where the tenant is responsible for paying their own utilities and a portion of the building's taxes, insurance, maintenance, and cleaning fees. The way this scenario plays out will be depend on a variety of factors including a building's location, amenities, traffic counts, area demographics, lease comparisons etc. as well as the negotiation skills of your commercial real estate agent.

Percentage

These kinds of leases are most prevalent in the retail industry. A percentage lease is one that allows the landlord to share in the profits of an establishment once the tenant reaches an agreed upon sales volume. To better illustrate this point, I've provided a sample percentage rent calculation below:

> **Monthly rent =**
> Base Rent + Percentage rent
> **Percentage rent =**
> Max [(gross sales – breakpoint), 0] * percentage

As you can see, percentage rent is only achieved if the tenant's gross sales exceed the *"breakpoint"*, the dollar value of sales agreed upon in the lease. For example, let's imagine a percentage lease calls for 5% in additional rent after gross sales of $750,000. If the tenant's sales volume reaches $950,000, the tenant will be required to pay an additional $10,000 in rent for the year (($950,000 – $750,000) *0.05). However, if the tenant only achieved a sales volume of $650,000, they wouldn't be responsible for paying any additional rent. Because a landlord has the potential to share in the tenant's profits, base rents for these agreements tend to be lower than some lease types.

Net-leases

These kinds of lease agreements are common for retail and industrial properties. A *"net lease"* is one that requires a tenant to pay, in addition to rent, some or all the property expenses that would normally be paid by the property owner. These expenses may include, but are not limited to, fixed operating expenses such as property taxes, insurance, and common area maintenance (C.A.M). There are three types of net leases which I've highlighted below:

Single-net (N)

A single net lease is one where tenants pay a set rent as well as a portion or all the property taxes for the building. Hence the single *"N"* in the lease name. The percentage of property taxes paid by the tenant is negotiated with the landlord prior to the lease being signed. Also, tenants are generally responsible for paying their own utilities and other services, such as internet, cell phone services etc. The landlord would be responsible for covering all other building expenses and repairs.

Double-net (NN)

A double net lease is like a single net lease, except the tenant also pays a portion or all the insurance premiums for the space. The tax and insurance percentages paid by the tenant are negotiated with the landlord prior to the lease being signed. Along with that, tenants are generally responsible for their own utilities and other services, such as internet, cell phone plans etc. The landlord would be responsible for covering all other building expenses and repairs.

Triple-net (NNN)

A triple-net lease is one where the tenant agrees to pay all real estate taxes, building insurance, and maintenance on the property. Along with that, the tenant is generally responsible for his/her own utilities and other services, such as internet, cell phone services etc. Although the landlord's responsibilities are limited, they're usually required to take maintain the roof and structure of the building.

However, using another kind of triple-net lease, called *"absolute triple-net"*, landlords can pass along the roof and structure responsibilities to the tenant. Absolute triple-net leases are most prevalent in *"single tenant net lease"* (S.T.N.L) properties such as Walgreens, McDonalds, Dunkin' Donuts, Starbucks etc.

Which should you pursue?

After reviewing the different types of commercial leases, one question remains, *"which lease agreement is right for you?"* Unfortunately, the answer to this question is *"it *depends*". The best agreement for your situation will be based on a variety of factors including:

- *What's your budget?*
- *Where would you like to be located?*
- *How much space do you need?*
- *How long of a lease are you willing to sign?*
- *What's your timeline on making a decision?*
- *What type of business do you own?*
- *Who's your target demographic?*
- *What types of leases are being offered for comparable buildings in your desired area?*
- *What is your projected sales volume over the next few years?*
- *As well as many more...*

For example, in the Louisville market, most industrial tenants sign net leases. Along with that, many local office tenants operate under either gross or modified gross leases. you pay will be based on what area of town you're in, the condition of the property and what comparable offerings in the area are advertising. Since these responses will be heavily influenced by your geographic area, I highly encourage you to lean on the expertise of your commercial real estate agent to help you navigate the process.

Action Items

1) Set aside time this week to familiarize yourself with each commercial lease type.

2) Work with your commercial real estate agent to get a feel for what lease types are available in your market given your business use.

3) Answer the questions provided in this section and get clear on what to expect during your property search.

CHAPTER 6
CALCULATING YOUR MONTHLY CASH OUTFLOW

"Never take your eyes off the cash flow because it's the life blood of business."
—**Sir Richard Branson**

This is probably one of the most common pitfalls I see business owners encounter when evaluating commercial properties. Commercial rents are calculated quite differently than those in a residential setting. Because of this, it's easy to misinterpret the financial commitment associated with leasing a commercial space.

Many business owners assume their base rent will be their only expense. However, this is often not the case. Other expenses may include a building's taxes, insurance, maintenance etc. As a result, it's important to discuss how to properly calculate your monthly *"cash outflow"*, which includes your base monthly rent as well as other property related expenses specified in your lease agreement.

Unlike residential real estate, the rent you pay for commercial space will depend on the total square footage defined in your lease agreement. Depending on the number of tenants and the amount of common area in the property, you may be quoted a *"Usable Square Footage"* (USF) or *"Rentable Square Footage"* (RSF). Below I've provided an overview of each:

Usable square footage (USF)

This is the term most business owners associate with leasing commercial space. Usable square footage (USF) describes the total area unique to the tenant. No other tenant has access to that space. If you're located in a single-tenant property, your lease agreement will likely reference USF. However, this is often not the case in a multitenant building. In these properties, tenants will often pay a portion of the operating expenses for the common areas based on their footprint in the building. This is where *"rentable square footage"* comes into play.

Rentable square footage (RSF)

This term is most used in lease agreements for multi-tenant office buildings as well as retail stores within shopping centers. Rentable square footage is described as the usable square footage plus a portion of a building's common area (i.e. hallways, public bathrooms, waiting areas etc.) To determine how much of a property's common area each tenant is responsible for, commercial landlords use a metric called the *"Load Factor"*. A property's load factor is calculated by dividing the building's total rentable square footage by its total usable square footage. To illustrate this point, I've provided the equation below:

> **Load Factor =**
> **(Rentable space/Usable space) - 1**

For example, if a building's rentable space is 220,000 and the usable space is 200,000, the property's load factor would be 10% ((220,000/200,000) – 1). To see how this ratio would apply in your lease analysis, let's imagine that you're comparing available space in two different office buildings. Both have the same usable space (10,000 SF) and rental rate. However, the load factor for each is 15% and 20% respectively. Therefore, the rentable space for each would be as follows:

> **Rentable space #1 =**
> **10,000 SF * 1.15 = 11,500 SF**
> **Rentable space #2 =**
> **10,000 SF * 1.20 = 12,000 SF**

As you can see, space #2 has 500 SF more rentable space than space #1. Therefore, if all other variables are equal, you would be better off leasing space in office building #1 because your monthly rent obligation would be lower.

Calculating Your Monthly Cash Outflow

Performing your rental analysis

Now that you've calculated your rentable space, it's time to determine your monthly rent obligation. Commercial lease rates are generally expressed on a *"price per square foot"* (p.s.f) basis. This metric represents the rent a tenant would expect to pay per square foot of space over the course of a year. To better illustrate this point, I've provided the equation below:

> **Yearly rent =**
> Space defined in lease agreement * price per square foot

For example, if the space defined in your lease agreement is 10,000 SF and your rental rate is $12 p.s.f., your yearly base rent would be:

> **Yearly Rent =**
> 10,000 SF * $12 p.s.f = $120,000 per year

In this scenario, your base rent would be $10,000 per month. However, this may not be the only cash outflow you have to account for. Depending on your commercial lease type, you may have to pay additional expenses such as your pro-rata share of the building's real estate taxes, insurance, and maintenance etc. In most commercial contracts, landlords define these additional expenses either:

1) **Net Charges** – will typically cover things like property maintenance, landscaping, site improvements, security,

taxes, common utilities, insurance payments and/or repairs. The amount you pay will be based on your footprint within the building.

2) **C.A.M Charges** – the costs associated with maintaining the common areas of a multi-tenant property. The amount you're responsible for paying is calculated by taking the total C.A.M charges and multiplying it by your pro-rata share of the building's leasable space.

For example, let's imagine that the previously mentioned space was marketed as a Triple-Net (NNN) lease. Under this agreement you would be responsible for paying taxes, insurance, and maintenance for the space. For simplicity sake, let's assume these net charges sum up to an additional $3 p.s.f. Below I've provided the corresponding calculation:

> **Yearly net charges =**
> 10,000 SF * $3 p.s.f = $30,000 per year

Given these additional charges, your monthly cash outflow for building related expenses would be:

> **Yearly outflow =**
> $120,000 + $30,000 = $150,000 per year
> **Monthly outflow =**
> $150,000/12 months = $12,500 per month

As you can see, failing to account for these additional charges would have left you $2,500 in the red each month!

Not only that, but other expenses such as utilities, internet, phone lines, trash pick-up etc. would put you further in the hole and leave you struggling to meet your obligations. As you review potential spaces, be sure to account for these additional expenses in your rental calculations. By doing so, you won't be caught off guard and will start your business on more solid financial footing.

> **Pro-tip:** Although p.s.f is generally expressed in a yearly rate, in states like California, p.s.f is listed as monthly. For this reason, it's crucial that you get clarification from your commercial real estate agent to ensure you understand how your base rent is calculated.

Action Items

1) Use the information provided in this section to calculate your usable/rentable space.
    a. Depending on your commercial lease type, your additional expenses will vary.
2) Once you determine your usable/rentable space, calculate your base rent by multiplying your usable/rentable space by your rental rate (p.s.f).
    a. Also consider your commercial lease type and account for any additional expenses related to the maintenance and operation of the building.
3) Review these numbers with your commercial real estate agent to see if they are in line with similar offerings in the market.

CHAPTER 7
SECURING YOUR NEW SPACE

"A big business starts small."
—**Richard Branson**

Now that you've laid out your criteria, learned about the different commercial lease types and determined how to calculate your monthly cash outflow, the real fun is about to begin! You're ready to start your search for a new space. Over the next few months, you will work with your commercial real estate agent to identify, review, and secure a commercial property. In this section, we'll outline the step-by step process you will follow to achieve this objective.

Identifying potential properties

As you begin your search, focus on identifying properties that meet the needs of your business. Review properties online via your local commercial real estate listing platform as well as national sites such as Crexi and LoopNet.

Second, consider driving around town and identifying signs that read, *"for rent"* and/or *"available for lease"*. If you find a space that you like, provide the contact information to your commercial real estate agent and have them call the owner on your behalf.

Third, stop by your local chamber of commerce and inquire about available space in your area. Often, they will have a directory of properties available for lease. If you're a chamber member and are willing to sign a long-term lease, they may be willing to offer you favorable terms to occupy the space.

Finally, reach out to your network via LinkedIn, Facebook, Instagram etc. and express your interest in leasing commercial space. Provide your criteria and timeline for wanting to move in. If your network is broad and diverse enough, you may have a connection or two who can point you in the right direction.

Reviewing your options

Once you and your commercial real estate agent compile a list of potential properties, set up appointments to view each one. If possible, schedule them on the same day or as close together as possible. This will ensure your memory is fresh so you can effectively compare them prior to making your final decision. As you tour each space, take pictures, and write detailed notes on what you see.

Whenever I tour a property, I organize the corresponding photos and notes in a folder on my google drive for easy access later. If the interior needs work, consider inviting a contractor to walk the property with you. That way, you're able to get an idea of what it would cost to make the interior functional for your use. Your commercial real estate agent should be able to provide you with a list of trustworthy contractors they've worked with in the past.

After completing the tours, sit down with your commercial real estate agent to discuss the pros and cons of each. Reference your *"must have's"* and *"nice to have's"* as well as your budget, space and location requirements. When I perform this analysis with my clients, we grade each from first to last based on how in-line they are with their criteria.

Submitting an L.O.I

Now that you've decided on a space, you'll need to draft and submit a *"Letter of Intent"* (L.O.I) to the landlord. A L.O.I is a non- binding document that proposes contract terms you're willing to accept. Since you're interested in leasing commercial space, the L.O.I will include references to your intended use, base rent, lease type, lease length, tenant improvement allowances, free rent etc. Your commercial real estate agent should be well-versed in drafting these documents and the language that should be present.

Along with that, you may be asked to provide a host of financial documents to the landlord. These may include bank statements, tax returns, profit & loss statements, balance sheets, credit reports, and more. As we highlighted in the *"Building Your Real Estate Advisory Team"* chapter, work with your accountant to compile these documents and ensure they are accurate. Although these are commonly requested items during lease negotiations, I'm often met with push back from my clients on their necessity. One of the most common objections I hear is *"Why does the landlord need to see my financials? I don't feel comfortable sharing them."*

Although I understand your hesitation, remember that landlords do not run a charity. They want to ensure you're financially able to fulfill your lease commitment if they decide to move forward with you as a tenant. Any supporting documentation you can provide your commercial real estate agent will help them better pitch you and your business to a prospective landlord. This is especially valuable in a competitive market where you may be competing against multiple business owners for the same space.

Once the landlord receives your L.O.I and supporting documentation, they can choose to either reject, counter or accept your offer. If the landlord counters or rejects your offer, you will either accept the revised terms, draw up a new counteroffer or walk away from the property. However, if they accept, you will enter contract negotiations for your new space. In the next section, we'll highlight some of the most important provisions to consider.

> **Pro-tip:** For a sample L.O.I that you can reference during future commercial transactions, check out the link provided here: https://bit.ly/2ZFOBeB.

Action Items

1) Employ the strategies discussed in this section to identify available properties that meet your criteria.
2) Tour each space and take pictures and detailed notes.
   a. If the space needs work, bring a general contractor along with you to provide insight on the build out that will be required.
3) Once you complete your viewings, sit down with your commercial real estate agent to narrow down your list.
   a. Reference your "must have's" and "nice to have's" list as well as your budget, location and space requirements.
4) Submit a L.O.I and supporting documentation to your prospective landlord.
   a. Remember, the more information you provide, the easier it will be for your commercial real estate agent to pitch you and your business to your prospective landlord.

CHAPTER 8
NEGOTIATING LEASE TERMS

"You cannot negotiate with people who say what's mine is mine and what's yours is negotiable."
—John F. Kennedy

You've finally made it to the negotiation table! However, now the real work begins. Going forward, you must work with your commercial real estate agent and real estate attorney to come to terms with your prospective landlord. Although this can be a contentious interaction, it doesn't have to be. In this section, we'll highlight how to maintain a proper mindset as well as explain some of the most relevant provisions to consider as you work on drafting the final lease agreement.

> **Disclaimer:** To be clear, I am not a lawyer, nor do I claim to be. The information provided in this section has been compiled based on my own personal experience, the experience of my clients and conversations I've had with legal professionals. If you have any questions and/or concerns regarding any of the content contained in this chapter, please seek the advice of a licensed real estate attorney.

Be willing to compromise

Although this is a simple concept, it's one that's often overlooked. I've met many business owners and investors who take the *"my way or the highway"* approach to negotiating. They're so rigid in their desires and are often unwilling to compromise. Because of this, the deal usually falls apart and both parties are left frustrated with the other. Understand that a lease negotiation is a two-way street. Both you and the landlord want to have their needs met. Therefore, to work out a deal that satisfies both parties, everyone in the transaction must be willing to compromise.

If your primary objective is to achieve the lowest rental rate possible, be open to taking the space *"as-is"* and not demanding significant rental concessions. Along with that, if the landlord is adamant about getting a specific term length, offer to sign a longer lease in exchange for lower base rent and/or increased rental concessions. As you go back and forth with the landlord, you will eventually settle on an agreement that's acceptable to both parties. Once you reach this point, avoid renegotiating every little detail. Remember, you will likely be occupying the space for multiple years. If you're overly aggressive during negotiations and try to squeeze every cent out of the transaction, your landlord will remember. As a result, they will likely be less open to accommodating your requests throughout your lease term. The moral of this story is to seek a mutually beneficial agreement that supports both yours and the landlord's goals. Trust me when I say, this type of agreement has the highest ROI.

Rental Rate

Probably the most hotly contested item in commercial lease negotiations is the rental rate. A common phrase I hear is *"I want to pay as little rent as possible for the space."* Although I understand this sentiment, how much you pay in rent depends on a variety of factors. For example, if you operate a plumbing business, your customers may not care where you set up shop. In this case, it may be wise to seek a lower rental rate so you can dedicate more resources towards marketing and purchasing tools to provide better service to your clients.

On the other hand, if you run a retail business, there may be instances where paying a little more each month is well worth it. If you own a restaurant, locating yourself in a heavily trafficked retail center could amplify your sales over time. Although the rent will be higher, you will likely make up for it in increased revenue.

Having said that, let's discuss a few ways to approach your negotiations to minimize your exposure to higher lease rates. First, you can propose taking the space *"as-is"* and limiting the number and size of rental concessions you request from the landlord. Since the landlord will have to invest less money on the front end, they may be more willing to reduce your rental rate.

Second, if you're open to signing a longer lease, your prospective landlord may be willing to lower the rental rate. Landlords prefer longer leases because it limits the risk of vacancy, thus, stabilizing their cashflow.

Finally, understand that this item is not the end all be all. You may still be able to work out a favorable lease agreement by conceding some on the rental rate in exchange for other concessions such as free/reduced rent, tenant improvement and furniture allowances, a shorter lease term etc. We'll discuss these items, as well as many more, throughout the rest of this chapter.

Lease term

The second item to consider is how long of a lease you're willing to sign. Generally, commercial leases run anywhere between 3-10 years, with some extending 20 or more years! Landlords prefer signing qualified tenants to long-term leases because it provides them with stable cashflows over a longer period. If you're willing to sign a longer lease, landlords will be more inclined to offer you incentives to move into the space.

Having said that, it's important to base your desired lease length on your long-term business goals. If you see yourself committing to an area for an extended period, you may opt for a longer lease term to lock in a lower rental rate. However, if you're a startup and don't yet have a proof of concept, it may be wise to pay a little more in rent each month to secure a shorter lease term. That way, you maintain flexibility and limit the downside risk if things don't go as planned with your business.

Lease concessions

In some instances, landlords may be willing to offer *"lease concessions"* to incentivize tenants to lease space in their building. Lease concessions are benefits landlords afford prospective tenants to entice them to sign a long-term lease. Some of the most common concessions in commercial real estate include:

- *Free Rent*
- *Reduced Rent*
- *Tenant Improvement Allowance (T.I.)*
- *Reduced Security Deposit*
- *Furniture allowance*
- As well as many more...

The incentives offered by landlords will be heavily influenced by current market conditions, your financial solvency, and offerings of similar properties in the area. If you have marginal financials and you want to lease space in a very desirable area, landlords will likely not offer much in the way of concessions. However, if you have strong financials and comparable properties are offering sizable concessions, you'll likely be in a stronger negotiating position. In either scenario, discuss this topic with your commercial real estate agent to determine which concessions to request.

Pro-tip: In situations where my client will need a few months to begin operations (i.e. finishing a build out, growing their customer base, waiting on a backlog of inventory etc.), I usually encourage them to ask for free rent or rent abatements on the front end of their lease. For example, if you're interested in signing a 3-year lease, consider asking for 4 months of free rent in exchange for signing a 40-month lease. That way, the landlord gets their 3-year lease and you get 4 months of runway to build up your cash reserves before paying your first month's rent.

Renewal options

This is probably one of the provisions I most often advocate for during lease negotiations. A renewal option gives the tenant the right to renew their lease agreement based on pre-determined terms. For example, let's imagine you sign a 3-year lease with two 3-year renewal options. During the first term, you agree to a base monthly rent of $5,000 with a 10% increase after each renewal. This means that if you choose to exercise your renewal options, your base monthly rent for each subsequent term would be $5,500 and $6,050 respectively.

The benefit of having multiple renewal options is that it puts you in the driver's seat. If at the end of your term the economy is doing well and market rates are high, you can lock in your renewal at the lower rate. On the other hand, if the economy is doing poorly and there are many vacant properties available, you can either renegotiate your existing terms or leave the space and sign a lease at a property in a better location and/or at a more favorable rate. During negotiations, you're better off opting for a shorter lease term with multiple renewal options. This allows you to reassess whether you want to remain in the space near the end of each term.

Exclusivity

This lease provision can be extremely important, especially if you're located in a multi-tenant building. An exclusivity clause is one that grants you exclusive right to engage in a certain type of activity at that location. For example, if you operate a liquor store in a shopping center, you likely don't want another one moving into the adjacent space. This is because having 2 liquor stores in such close proximity would be bad for business. Therefore, you'll want to ask for the exclusivity of being the only liquor store allowed on the premises.

It's not uncommon for landlords of multi-tenant properties to give qualified tenants an exclusivity of use. Having said that, its specificity is an item you'll need to negotiate. The broader the verbiage, the more favorable it is for the tenant because more businesses fall under the umbrella. On the other hand, if the exclusivity clause is too specific, you may find yourself becoming neighbors with one of your competitors.

However, there are instances where having exclusivity may hurt you. For example, restaurants that are located close to each other tend to outperform those that are isolated and away from other dining options. For that reason, it's important to consider various scenarios to ensure you're making the right decision based on your business type.

Right of first refusal

If you plan on leasing space in a multi-tenant office, retail and or industrial property, you'll want to include this provision in the final contract. In commercial real estate, a right of first refusal gives you the right to enter into a lease agreement for vacant space within the building before anyone else. If the landlord offers you the space and you decline to match their terms, they are free to entertain other offers.

For example, let's imagine you occupy 2,000 SF in a 6,000 SF multi-tenant retail center. You have the right of first refusal on the adjacent 2,000 SF space and it is currently sitting vacant. After 3 months, a prospective tenant approaches the landlord with an L.O.I to fill the vacancy. Since you hold a right of first refusal on the adjacent space, the landlord must give you an opportunity to match the terms. From there, you could choose to either lease the space at the proposed terms or decline to exercise your right. The benefit of having this provision in place is that it gives you the option to expand in the future. Given the monetary and non-monetary costs associated with moving from a location, you're usually better off expanding operations at your current address.

Subleasing

This is a provision I always recommend my clients fight to include in their lease. Although business owners go into their tenancy thinking they're going to see it through to the end, things don't always go as planned. Maybe demand for your product or service sharply increases and you soon outgrow your space. On the other hand, maybe your business struggles to get off the ground and you're forced to downsize or completely shut down operations. In either scenario, you want to have the option to relieve yourself from having to pay rent and other building related expenses for a space you're no longer utilizing. This is where a *"sublease"* provision comes into play.

A sublease clause is one that affords you the right to lease your space to a third party in the event you need to leave your current location. Having said that, most landlords will not give you free reign to sublease to whomever you choose. They will likely require them to be of equal or higher financial standing than you and your business. As a result, your landlord will usually request documentation and financial records proving this fact.

Along with that, subleasing your space does not absolve you of all responsibility for the lease. You will still be responsible for complying with all the lease terms as well as collecting rent from the sublessor and remitting payment to the landlord. In essence, you become the landlord to the sublessor. If your sub-tenant does not comply with the terms laid out in the agreement, you may be held responsible for fulfilling the lease obligations. For that reason, it's important to properly vet potential sublessors to ensure this scenario doesn't come to fruition.

Landlord and tenant responsibilities

Regardless of what business you're in, this item is one you will need to give some thought to. Depending on which commercial lease type is being marketed, landlords and tenants will likely already have their responsibilities spelled out in the contract.

However, if the market warrants it, I often recommend that my clients request that some, if not all, responsibility of *"big ticket items"* such as maintenance and repair of the roof, structure, HVAC systems, elevators, boiler/water heater etc. be assigned to the landlord. The reason for this is that when these components fail, it can cost thousands of dollars to remedy! For most small businesses, this kind of financial hit would be crippling.

Having said that, you may find yourself in a situation where the landlord is adamant about passing along these responsibilities to you as the tenant. In these instances, consider proposing a cap on expenses each year. This helps limit the downside risk of replacing a major component during your tenancy.

For example, in June 2020, I helped a business owner secure a favorable lease to open an international grocery store. As part of the agreement, we were able to negotiate a $500 yearly cap on maintenance and repair of the HVAC system. If the HVAC system were to break down, my client would only have to pay up to $500 and the rest would be covered by the landlord. Given the cost of a new commercial HVAC system would be more than $7,500, this clause will save her a lot of heartache.

Performing a commercial property inspection

This is an especially important action item to complete if you're responsible for maintaining the interior and exterior of your commercial space. A commercial property inspection is one where *"an inspector collects information through visual observation during a walk-through survey of the subject property, conducting research about the property, and then generating a meaningful report about its condition"*. The reason conducting an inspection is so important is because it limits the risk of you coming out of pocket to replace and/or repair any of the property's *"big-ticket items"* including:

- *HVAC system*
- *Water Heater*
- *Elevators*
- *Boilers*
- *Roof & Siding*
- *Structure*
- *As well as many more...*

As you begin your search for a property inspector, make sure they're well versed in inspecting commercial buildings. Unlike residential real estate where most of the building components are similar, commercial buildings vary widely. Depending on the building's usage, the inspector may need to inspect commercial lifts, bay doors, restaurant components, elevators etc. If they don't know what to look out for, it could spell big trouble for you and your business. Given the level of knowledge required to properly perform these inspections, commercial property inspections tend to cost more than residential ones. Having said that, the few extra hundred dollars in cost could save you thousands over your lease term.

Carefully review each item

Once you and the landlord have agreed to terms, THROUGHLY review the final contract. Remember that once you sign your name on the dotted line, you're agreeing to EVERYTHING that is written in the document. Double and triple check the language, envision potential pitfalls and highlight sentences within the contract that you want clarification on. If you don't feel comfortable with any of the contract language, send the contract to your real estate attorney for review. They will provide you with the appropriate language to ensure that your best interests are represented in the agreement.

Pro tip: Commercial leases are often written to favor the landlord/lessor, not the lessee. Because of this, I recommend having your real estate advisory team review the lease prior to signing on the dotted line. The first person to consult should be your commercial real estate agent. As a disclaimer, unless they're licensed to practice law, they will be unable to offer you any legal advice. However, they can tell you whether certain provisions within the lease are common in the market, which ones you should consider renegotiating and/or whether to seek legal advice. Once they've had a chance to review it, send the revised draft to your real estate attorney for final review. Although it will cost you to have them look at the contract, a few hundred dollars spent on the front end could save you thousands of dollars over your lease term.

Action Items

1) *Enter lease negotiations with an open mind and be willing to compromise on some items.*
   a. *Remember, you want to maintain a good relationship with your landlord going forward. Therefore don't be overly aggressive and/or nit-pick every little detail within the contract.*
2) *Get clear on what you want to accomplish in the agreement and how the terms will best support your business.*
   a. *Your commercial real estate agent should clarify what to expect and how to approach your negotiations.*
3) *If possible, pass along responsibility for the "big-ticket items" to the landlord.*
   a. *If the landlord won't budge, consider requesting a cap on expenses to limit the downside risk of replacing one of these expensive components.*
4) *Once you agree to terms, CAREFULLY REVIEW THE FINAL CONTRACT!*
   a. *Remember, once you sign your name on the dotted line, you're agreeing to everything that's written in that document.*
   b. *If you're not comfortable with some of the language, seek the services of a competent real estate attorney.*

CHAPTER 9
COMPLETING YOUR BUILD-OUT

"You are actually constructing what your head understood about what your eyes saw."
—**Doris McCarthy**

Congratulations on finally agreeing to terms with your landlord! You're one step closer to making your entrepreneurial dream a reality. Although some commercial spaces are move-in ready, others may require interior modification. Sometimes, the prior tenant's use is completely unrelated to yours and thus, you will need to perform a *"build-out"*. In this section, we'll explain how to identify and work with a stellar general contractor who will modify your space to ensure it's functional for your intended use.

Why hire a general contractor?

A general contractor (GC) is a professional who is responsible for the day-to-day oversight of a construction site, management of vendors and trades, and the communication of information to all involved parties throughout the course of a building project. Hiring a reputable and competent GC takes the pressure of managing a construction project off you and allows you to focus your attention on getting your business up and running.

However, since GC's usually charge a fee for their services, many of my cost-conscious clients ask, *"Why should I hire a GC if I can contract out the work myself and save money?"*. Renovating commercial space can be a laborious and stressful process. As an example, if you're looking to convert a retail space into a functional restaurant in Louisville, KY, here are just some of the items you'll need to address:

- *Installing a 3 – compartment sink.*
- *Installing hand sink(s) that are accessible to workstations.*
- *Ensuring there is hot and cold water with sufficient pressure.*
- *Installing a waste-tank that's 50% or larger than your freshwater tank.*
- *Installing refrigeration unit (s) that register temperatures of 41°F or below.*
- *Fitting the space with the proper electrical work to ensure your equipment functions as intended.*
- *Adding or tearing down walls to create a functional layout.*
- *Installing proper ventilation to ensure hot air is escaping the kitchen correctly.*
- *As well as many more...*

For this job alone, you would need to hire electricians, plumbers, drywall contractors, concrete contractors, roofers

Before You Sign That Lease...

etc. Coordinating all these individuals and ensuring the work is done properly and on time can be a stressful and cumbersome experience. Instead of focusing your efforts in this area, you would be better served addressing other business-related items to ensure you're ready to begin operations once construction is complete.

Getting clear on your construction budget

Now that you understand the value of a stellar GC, you'll need to address your total construction budget. Depending on the terms of your lease agreement, your landlord may allocate a certain dollar amount towards a *"tenant improvement allowance"* (T.I.). Tenant improvement allowance is an amount the landlord credits new tenants for costs associated with renovating the space. Any work done at or under this amount is 100% paid for by the landlord. If you have a T.I. allowance, it would be wise to use it when making your renovations. Having said that, you will likely have to front the money for construction and have the landlord reimburse you at the end. If this is the case, ensure you have ample funds in place to account for these costs as well as other bills during construction.

If you don't have any tenant improvement funds available, perform a financial analysis to determine how much you can allocate towards renovating your space. If you're a start-up, it's usually wise to maintain between 3-6 months of working capital to account for startup costs as well as building up your clientele. Any extra capital above that amount can be used to renovate your existing space.

If you lack any excess funds, consider seeking financing from other sources. Often, there are local government programs that offer low-cost financing options for small businesses. In the Louisville market, two of the most beneficial are those provided by *"Louisville Forward"* and *"Navigate Enterprise Center"*. Louisville Forward, the Metro Government's economic development department, has helped hundreds of people start and grow small businesses in Louisville. They, along with Navigate Enterprise Center, issue small business loans to entrepreneurs who want to purchase equipment, supplies, raw materials, and/or secure space to conduct their business operations.

Along with that, local and regional banks usually have small business financing available for business owners interested in purchasing equipment and funding build outs for their space. Although they're often more stringent than comparable public offerings, their loan terms can be equally, if not more competitive than the alternatives. If you're located in an urban area, you will likely have similar public and private offerings to explore. Work with your accountant and commercial real estate agent to review these options and select one that best supports your business goals.

Choosing your general contractor

With your construction budget in hand, it's time to identify potential GC candidates. To start, ask your commercial real estate agent if they know anyone they would recommend. Your agent will likely have worked with multiple commercial contractors in the past and will be happy to provide you with a list of vetted professionals. Along with that, ask other business owners in your social sphere if they know of any good commercial contractors. Like you, many business owners have used commercial contractors in the past to modify their existing space. If they had a good experience with one, they will likely recommend them to you. Finally, search online to find the best rated ones in your area. When reading their reviews, look for references to the quality of their work, their responsiveness, timeliness, and ability to stay on budget. These characteristics, along with many others, are ones that all great commercial contractors possess.

It's important to note that you need to verify that the contractor you work with is licensed and bonded in the state where the work will be performed. Although individuals who aren't may offer a better price, it's often not worth the risk. Licensed general contractors are held to a high ethical standard and are required to maintain insurance policies that cover them if any legal actions are taken against them. As a result, it will be much easier to collect damages if issues arise during the project and you're forced to file a complaint against them. Once you've compiled a list of at least 5 potential candidates, interview each one. Some of the questions to consider asking include:

1) *Do you have prior experience with these types of projects?*
2) *How do you manage your scheduling?*

3) Can you give me a timeline on the work that needs to be done?
4) Will you be my contact person during the project?
    a. If not, does my contact have experience with similar projects?
5) How do you handle site supervision?
6) How much will I need to put down?
    a. If the contractor wants more than half the money up front, be wary. Most reputable contractors will likely only request enough to cover the initial material costs for the job.
7) What else should I be asking you?

Like the other professionals you hired, get clear on how you will communicate with them as well as the frequency with which you will do so. Renovating a commercial space is an in-depth process that requires constant communication between you and your GC. If you prefer to communicate via text and email, make sure they're comfortable using those mediums as well. After interviewing each one, select your top 3 candidates.

> **Pro-tip:** Like the rest of your real estate advisory team, it's important to verify that your general contractor has experience completing commercial construction projects. Although residential GC's can perform the work, they're often unaware of the many nuances associated with building out a commercial space. This increases the chances of an error occurring which will cost you time and money to remedy. Along with that,

> they likely won't have established relationships with the appropriate sub-contractors who will help bring the project to a successful completion. Just like you wouldn't hire an auto mechanic for fix a jet engine, don't hire a residential contractor to perform a commercial buildout.

Getting bids for the work

Now that you have a list of your top choices, request that each provide you with a construction bid. The reason I recommend 3 separate bids is because it gives you an idea of what the market rate is for the work you would like completed. After receiving the bids, scrutinize each one. If you don't understand why a line item is necessary, ask for clarification on its necessity. Sometimes, contractors charge for work that's above and beyond what you want completed. If this is the case, you can choose to either remove the line item, perform the task yourself and/or defer the work to a later date.

Although it may be tempting to choose the discount contractor, I often recommend my clients select the middle quote. This is because a discounted price is often a reflection of their lack of proper experience and/or a track record of success. More often than not, the middle quote is one that properly compensates the general contractor for their experience while not building in the fluff charged by much larger contractors with significant overhead (i.e. employees, a large office lease etc.).

Once you select your contractor, consider adding 10-15% on top of your quote to account for any delays and/or issues that may arise during the project. Regardless of how great your GC is, it's impossible to predict the future. Therefore, factoring in a buffer amount will help mitigate the issues that may arise throughout the renovation.

> **Pro-tip:** Unlike residential construction, commercial construction projects often have a higher price tag. For that reason, understand you will likely experience some sticker shock when you see these commercial quotes for the first time. If you're handy, consider doing some of the work yourself. Although your landlord will likely require you to hire a licensed contractor to perform much of the extensive work such as the electrical, HVAC, plumbing etc., you can save hundreds if not thousands of dollars by performing less complex tasks on your own. Examples of these jobs may include doing your own demo work, painting, and priming walls, changing lighting fixtures etc.

Sticking to your timeline and budget

Once you've selected your commercial contractor, sit down with them to clearly define a project timeline for the work that needs to be done. If your contractor is experienced, they will likely create a visual representation of this timeline, known as a *"Gantt chart"*, to provide more clarity. A Gantt chart is one that depicts the project work to be completed over various stages of the project life cycle. To better illustrate this document, I've provided an example below:

As you can see, the type of activity, start date, duration and end date of each step are provided. This ensures that everyone is on the same page and that the expectations are clearly defined. Once the project begins, continually check-in to make sure you're on track to hit the target completion date. Periodically swing by the job site at different times of the day to see how the work is progressing. If you see something out of the ordinary, bring it to the attention of your GC. Although most great contractors will have a handle on this, you need to take an active role to ensure the project it stays on track.

If issues do arise, work with your GC to remedy the situation. This may include updating the Gantt chart to reflect delays and/or coordinating with new sub-contractors to perform the work. Finally, if your GC continually fails to address your concerns and proves themselves incapable of getting the job done, it may be wise to terminate the contract and move on to another candidate. Although this may be a difficult conversation to have, it's better to cut your losses and move on. Remember, if you properly vet your commercial GC on the front-end, you will likely avoid having to deal with this scenario.

> **Pro-tip:** I recommend structuring the agreement with your GC whereby the disbursements are issued whenever a milestone is hit on the project timeline. This helps limit the risk of them receiving most of the money upfront and not completing the work. For example, if you begin a $100,000 renovation for a retail store, you may provide $20,000 to your GC up-front to purchase materials and hire the initial subcontractors. Once they reach the next milestone and you're satisfied with the quality of their work, you would make the next disbursement. This would continue until the project is complete and the final disbursement is issued.

Action Items

1) Sit down and create a construction budget for the work that needs to be done to your space.
2) Interview at least 5 general contractors and select the top 3 from the list.
    a. Make sure you agree on how you will communicate with them.
3) Request bids from each of your top candidates and scrutinize each line item.
    a. If some of the items aren't contributing to making the space functional for your use, consider removing them from the quote.
    b. If you're cost-conscious and handy, consider doing some of the less complex work yourself.
    c. Remember, the middle quote is often the best one because it properly compensates an experienced general contractor for their work while eliminating the fluff charged by larger commercial contractors due to their increased overhead.
4) Regularly communicate with your GC to ensure that the project remains on time and on budget.

CHAPTER 10
TYING UP LOOSE ENDS

"What kind of competitor sees the finish line and slows down... always finish strong!"
—Gary Ryan Blair

As your renovations are underway, there are likely a few outstanding items you need to address prior to beginning operations. Depending on your use, these can vary widely. For this reason, it's important to do your own independent research to ensure you're addressing all the necessary action items prior to opening your doors. In this section we will discuss some of the most common as well as provide strategies you can use to streamline the process of completing each one.

Attaining proper licensing & permits

Regardless of what business you're in, you will likely be required to secure permits and/or licenses to operate. The most common and widely used is a *"business license"*. In the U.S., all businesses must secure a business license to operate legally. This is because states must be able to identify your business so they can track of your finances for tax purposes as well as ensure you're held accountable for your actions.

To secure your business license, google your city's name followed by the words *"business license"* and/or check the US Small Business Administration (SBA)'s website for details. Often you can simply follow the application procedures laid out on your state government's website or go to city hall and pick them up in person. You'll need to renew this license periodically, so track the deadlines by setting a reminder in your calendar.

Other required licenses and permits will depend on what industry you're in. For example, if you plan on opening a restaurant, you'll need food service licenses, food handler's permits and potentially a liquor license if you plan on serving liquor on site. If you operate a logistics company that utilizes semi-trucks, you'll likely need transportation/logistics permits to operate oversized and overweight vehicles. Because of this variability, it's important to do your own independent research to determine what permits and licenses are required for your industry. For a helpful article on this topic, I've provided a link below:

Licenses & Permits: https://bit.ly/2ETUBZC

Creating signage for your business

Although this section applies to all industries, it's especially important if you have a retail component to your business. The benefit of having signage on site is that it alerts potential customers that you're open for business. If you're located along a high traffic roadway, having a well-placed and attention-grabbing sign can translate into significant foot-traffic for your business. Although it would be nice to hang a sign wherever you please, cities usually have regulations that dictate where signs can be placed on the premises, their height and width as well as how high they can be off the ground.

To gather this information, call city hall and/or visit their website. Since they're the ones responsible for issuing signage permits, they will provide you with up to date information on what rules apply to your unique situation. Having said that, I generally recommend my clients cut out the middleman and call various sign companies around town. Since sign companies create and hang signs for a living, they often know exactly what is and isn't allowed in any given area around town. Not only that, but you're able to compile multiple bids and see which company offers you the best price and quality of service.

Securing commercial insurance

Depending on the type of commercial lease you sign, you may be responsible for securing insurance for your space. When it comes to insurance, it pays to shop around. However, identifying multiple insurance carriers and getting quotes from each can be extremely time consuming. For that reason, I often recommend my clients solicit the services of a competent and qualified *"commercial insurance broker"*.

Commercial insurance brokers are individuals who work with you to determine your insurance needs and shop a host of different carriers to get you the appropriate coverage for the best possible rate. There are a few benefits to using one.

First, they save you a significant amount of time. An experienced commercial insurance broker will have a long list of insurance carriers they've worked with in the past. Because of their familiarity with each carrier's offerings, they can streamline the review process and help you select the best coverage much faster than you could on your own.

Second, because they have pre-existing relationships with these carriers, you may get a much better price than shopping direct. Insurance companies often provide brokers with lower rates because they are professionally trained to accurately assess risk. As a result, a broker's clients usually present a lower risk to the carrier than those who secure insurance independently.

Third, they will be your point of contact for all your insurance related questions. Unlike large insurance companies that are known for being impersonal and difficult to get ahold of, your insurance broker will be available to answer your questions any time of day. I've had clients who have contacted their broker on nights and weekends. They received a prompt response, and the issues were resolved soon thereafter. If your commercial insurance broker is committed, they'll be there for you when you need them most.

Finally, they are 100% free for you to use! Like your commercial real estate agent, your commercial insurance broker is paid a commission by the carrier they ultimately pair you with. This means that you get the benefit of working with an expert in the insurance industry, without having to pay for their services. It's really a no brainer.

To find a great commercial insurance broker, start by asking your commercial real estate agent if they have any recommendations. Since they deal in the commercial arena every day, they will likely have a few they can refer to you. Along with that, ask your friends who are small business owners. If they're happy with their insurance broker, they will happily refer them to you. Once you have a list of potential candidates, call each one and ask them to provide you with a list of carriers they work with. Compare the lists, identify 2 agents who have differing carriers, and ask them to compile quotes for you. From there, choose the one who offers you the appropriate coverage for the best rate.

Action Items

1) *Register for a business license and do research on what other licenses and/or permits your business needs to legally operate.*
    a. *Maintaining these licenses and/or permits will likely be a recurring expense. Because of this, make sure you have funds set aside in your budget to cover these expenses.*
2) *Call at least 3 different sign companies and request bids from each.*
    a. *Along with that, ask them to confirm what you can and can't do on your property.*
3) *Ask your commercial real estate agent and other business owners who they recommend as a commercial insurance broker.*
    a. *Call each one and ask them to provide you with a list of carriers they affiliate with.*
    b. *Compare the lists and select 2 brokers who have differing carriers.*
    c. *Have each provide you with bids and choose the one that offers you the appropriate coverage for the best rate.*

CHAPTER 11
IMPLEMENTING A MARKETING STRATEGY

"Marketing strategy is a series of integrated actions leading to a sustainable competitive advantage."
—**John Sculley**

To succeed in business, you need a constant flow of customers who are ready, willing, and able to buy your goods/services. To attract these types of clients, you must actively market your offerings to them. As a result, it's important to implement a marketing strategy that's tailored to attract your target audience. Below I've provided a few strategies to help you accomplish this goal.

Social media

First, consider creating accounts on various social media platforms, including but not limited to, Facebook, Instagram, YouTube, LinkedIn etc. Not only are these platforms 100% free for you to use, but the engagement you can generate can be immense. In 2019, just over 72% of US adults admitted to having at least one social media account.

Of those individuals, over 60% said they used social media at least once per day[1]. Not only that, but according to 2018 report issued by PwC, 37% of consumers rely on social media as part of their purchasing process[2]. Because of this, the more times you get your marketing message in front of your target audience the higher the likelihood you have of converting them into paying customers.

As for strategies you can implement to maximize your initial exposure, consider creating content related to the progress you've made towards opening for business. For example, as you go through the leasing process, take pictures and videos documenting your experiences. If you're building out your space, create content showing the progress you've made and share your insights on the work. Ask your audience to provide feedback and individually thank those who participate in the discussion. Sharing these messages with your audience helps build engagement and increases the likelihood that they will share your story with others and/or become customers themselves.

Direct mail marketing

Although this method does require a bit of upfront capital, it can be one of the most effective. According to the *"Data & Marketing Association"* mailers were 9 times more effective at soliciting a response from a prospect than email. Not only that, since 2015, response rates for mailers have jumped by over 140%[3]! This is due, in large part, to businesses shifting much of their new business development activities online.

As for the cost of mailers, they can range from as little as $0.30 for a small postcard to as much as $10 for books, large colorful pamphlets etc. Depending on your industry and the lifetime value of your customers, the best mailers to use may vary. However, I usually recommend starting out with postcards because you can send hundreds out each month for a relatively small amount of money. When determining who to send to, you can either use your own list of existing clients or work with a *"list broker"* to compile a list of targeted prospects. Although this is beyond the scope of this book, I have provided additional information on how to identify, screen and work with a list broker here: https://bit.ly/3lE7mZ1

As part of your first campaign, consider mailing 500-1000 post cards to your target audience. With an average response rate of between 0.5 - 2%, you will usually get a few calls and/or visits each month from interested parties. However, more than likely, it will take at least a few attempts to get a response. Therefore, to get the best results, commit to sending postcards to the same list for at least 6-8 months. Consistency is key with mailing campaigns and by sticking to it for a period, you'll maximize your results.

In my business, I use *"Postcard Mania"* to market my services to prospective business owners and investors. Each month, I send around 2,000 postcards to landlords of multifamily and retail properties in the Louisville area. Since starting this campaign back in June of 2020, I've had a response rate of roughly 0.5%. This translates to around 10 new leads of potential clients who are interested in my offerings. Given the high lifetime value of a client in the commercial real estate brokerage business, even a 5% conversion rate translates to a significant return on investment.

Asking for reviews online

This one simple strategy is an absolute game changer for business owners. Every time you sell a product and/or service, ask your customer to review your business online. Google is the #1 search engine in the world, and it's often the first-place people go to when searching for a product and/or service. Because of this, prospective customers often put a lot of weight on online reviews prior to making a buying decision.

In fact, research shows that 91% of people regularly or occasionally read online reviews, and 84 percent trust online reviews as much as a personal recommendation. Along with that, 68 percent of respondents said they form an opinion after reading between one and six online reviews[4]. As a result, the more positive reviews you have, the more a prospective client will trust your brand.

Online reviews also help place you higher in the search rankings on Google. According to a study performed by a company called *"Local SEO"*, positive online reviews were shown to be *"a strong signal to search engines that communicates trustworthiness and authority"*.

Since the start my real estate career in 2019, I've made it a goal to ask each one of my clients to leave a review on our company website and my own real estate website. By committing to this strategy, I've been able to secure many favorable reviews that reference our integrity, hard work and dedication to helping our clients achieve their commercial real estate goals. Whether you do it via email, over the phone or in-person, don't forget to consistently ask for the review. Although not everyone will comply with your request, each positive review will compound your results over time.

Joining local associations, organizations, and groups

Although this strategy may not pay dividends right away, its one that can have a lasting impact on your business. Success in business is directly correlated to the quantity and quality of relationships you develop over time. The more positive relationships you foster with people in your industry and community, the more likely you are to convert a portion of them into clients and/or strategic partners. Therefore, investing time, energy, and resources into developing these relationships can be of great value to you.

To start, consider joining associations/organizations such as your local chamber of commerce, business networking groups, industry specific clubs, charitable organizations etc. When I began my career in commercial real estate, I decided to expand my network by joining one of the top *"Business Networking International"* (B.N.I) groups in the city of Louisville, KY. With over 270,000 members and 9,500 chapters worldwide, B.N.I is the world's leading referral organization[6]. The mission of B.N.I. is to help its members grow their businesses by creating an organized referral marketing system that leverages the relationships of all its members. For example, if you own a marketing agency and someone you know is looking for a plumber, you can refer them to the plumber in your BNI group. Likewise, if another member has a connection who is seeking to hire a marketing agency, they will refer them to you. This year, our group has generated over $2.5 million dollars in business for its members and will likely eclipse that number in the years to come.

Second, becoming involved with your local chamber of commerce can open opportunities for you and your business. A city's chamber of commerce is comprised of members who are dedicated to furthering the interests of businesses within their community. They organize events, advocate for pro-business legislation, and provide informational resources members can use to effectively grow their businesses.

Contrary to popular belief, your city's chamber of commerce doesn't only work with established businesses. In fact, if you're starting a new venture, you can work with them to plan an opening ceremony. They love supporting business owners who create jobs within the community. Therefore, they will leverage their strategic relationships with local media outlets and other members to market your grand opening around town. This can help you start your business off on the right foot and increase your likelihood of success long-term.

Finally, consider joining organizations that support causes you believe in. Not only will this satisfy your desire to help others, it can also help you develop strategic relationships with heavy hitters within your community. Most leaders and successful business owners are altruistic. As a result, they are generally active members of organizations that support charitable causes. If you establish yourself as a leader within these organizations, you'll garner a high level of trust which could lead to business opportunities in the future. Since 2018, I have been actively involved in the leadership of various local associations and organizations including:

1) **Junior Achievement** – *a global non-profit youth organization that partners with local businesses, schools and organizations to deliver experiential learning programs about work readiness, financial literacy and entrepreneurship.*

2) **Sigma Phi Epsilon Alumni Board** – *The alumni board tasked with supporting the University of Louisville's undergraduate chapter of Sigma Phi Epsilon fraternity.*

3) **Toastmaster International** – *a US non-profit educational organization that operates clubs worldwide for the purpose of promoting communication, public speaking, and leadership.*

Not only has volunteering for these organizations been extremely fulfilling, it has also afforded me the opportunity to network with community leaders as well as develop leadership and communication skills that will serve me well in the future. Set aside time this week to identify associations, organizations and groups that can help you grow professionally and personally. Commit to visiting a few and determine if they align with your business and personal goals. Remember, the more strategic relationships you develop with members of your community, the more likely you are to achieve success in business.

Action Items

1) Create business pages on various social media platforms including Facebook, Instagram, LinkedIn, YouTube etc.
    a. Regularly upload photo and video content documenting your experiences as you go through the process of opening for business.
2) If your lifetime value of a new customer is high, consider incorporating a direct mail campaign into your marketing strategy.
    a. Track your responses and adjust the post card's verbiage and offerings to increase response rates.
3) Become an active member of local associations, chamber of commerce and business networking groups.
    a. Regularly attend functions and contribute to the group.
    b. Consider taking on a leadership role and committing to personal development.
    c. Work with other group members to spread the word about your business.

CHAPTER 12
OPENING YOUR DOORS!

"It's when you take that first step to opening a business or making an investment that it becomes real." —**Robert Kiyosaki**

Congratulations on making it to the finish line! You're now ready to open your doors to the public. If you've followed the steps laid out in this book, you should have made it to this point relatively unscathed. However, now the real work is about to begin. For the rest of your time in business, you must effectively manage your operation to support your family, develop your team members and make a positive impact in your community. Although this is not a comprehensive list, below I've provided some of the most common real estate related items to consider throughout your lease term.

Complying with the terms of your lease

For as long as you operate at your location, you will need to comply with the terms laid out in your commercial lease agreement. However, because many commercial lease agreements are 10+ pages long and contain a plethora of legal jargon that's difficult to understand, business owners often struggle to identify what is expected of them as a tenant. Because of this, I usually sit down with my clients to create a simplified list that contains the most important items/dates within the lease agreement that they need to be aware of. Below, I've provided some of the most common items:

- **Rental Payment** – The amount of base rent due each month.
- **C.A.M Expenses** – Expenses associated with the maintenance of a property's common areas.
- **Additional Rent** – Most often used in percentage leases. References the additional rent that is due given the revenue generated by the business within a particular time frame.
- **Payment Dates** – Dates that your base rent, additional rent and/or CAM expenses are due.
- **Late Fees** – Any fees associated with paying your rent late.
- **Landlord Address** – The address where you send correspondence to your landlord. You generally need to provide written notice for renewing your lease, requesting repairs, subletting your space etc.
- **Notice Date** – This date refers to the deadline for offering notice to your landlord about renewing your lease. This date is usually between 3-12 months prior to your lease expiration date.

Once your list is complete, print and hang it up in your office and/or somewhere you can regularly see it. This ensures the information stays front of mind so you can respond accordingly when the situation calls for it. Also if you ever have questions regarding your lease agreement, reach out to your commercial real estate agent for clarification. They regularly deal with these agreements and will happily answer any real estate question you may have or refer you to a great real estate attorney if the question is outside of their purview.

Maintaining clear financial records

This is one of the most important items on the list and for good reason. According to a study performed by *"US Bank"*, 45% of businesses shutter their doors within the first 5 years of operation. Not only that, but of those businesses that close, 82% cite their reason for closure as *"poor cash flow management skills/poor understanding of cash flow"*[7]. Your *"cash-flow"* is the total amount of money being transferred into and out of your business. If you don't effectively track and manage cash within your business, it will likely spell trouble for you because you run the risk of not having enough money to meet your financial obligations. To maintain a firm understanding of your business's financial health, you must develop systems to efficiently track the movement of money within your business.

When starting out, use software programs like *"QuickBooks"* to manage and track revenue, invoices, payroll, maintenance expenses etc. Schedule a day each month to input invoices, receivables, payroll information as well as a host of other financial data into the system. By regularly updating your records, you will be able to generate accurate reports that provide an overview of your business's financial performance and highlight areas of improvement.

If this activity seems like something that would make your head spin, you can hire professionals, called *"book-keepers"*, who can manage this process for you. Their job is to keep detailed ledgers and records of the financial affairs of your business. Along with that, some may offer you advice on ways to conserve costs, increase revenue and various other actions that can help improve the financial health of your business.

Audit your shared expenses

This item is especially relevant if you occupy space within a multi-tenant building. In most instances, shared expenses, such as *"Net Charges"* and *"C.A.M expenses"*, will be assessed on a pro- rata basis. This means that the amount you pay will be based on your footprint within the building. Although this is generally appropriate, you'll want to verify that the amount you're required to pay is not negatively impacted by other tenants in the building. For example, if the water bill is shared but there is a hair salon and dog groomer on site, they will likely use more water than the average retail tenant. As a result, you should work with your landlord to confirm they are paying their fair share of the water bill and not passing along extra expenses to you and/or other tenants. Review these shared expenses periodically to ensure this remains valid.

Planning your future

As a passionate and driven entrepreneur, your future business goals likely include expanding your operations and positively impacting as many lives as possible. Because of this, it's important to create and regularly review your 1,3,5 and 10-year goals to determine how your real estate needs will evolve. If you're located in a multi-tenant building, consider negotiating a *"right of first refusal"* on any adjacent space. This will afford you the opportunity to expand your footprint within the building without having to move locations. If you're located in a stand-alone building, read your local business journal to keep abreast of new real estate trends. Along with that, periodically check-in with your commercial real estate agent. Not only will they provide you with an update on the real estate market, they will also happily refer you to anyone in their network who can help your business grow and succeed.

Keep in touch

Now that you've made it to the end of this book, be sure to keep us in mind for your future real estate needs! If you're located in Louisville, KY and its surrounding areas, I'd be honored to help you identify, analyze, negotiate and secure your next commercial space. You can contact me via email at raphael@grisantigroup.com and/or my cell at (502) 536-7315.

Even if you're not located in Louisville, I encourage you to reach out anyway! I'd be happy to share whatever insights I have as well as connect you with high-performing professionals in your area who can help you secure a commercial space that's right for you. I wish you and your business continued success in the future!

> **Note from the author:** If you enjoyed this book, I would greatly appreciate if you could leave a 5-star review on Amazon. Reviews are gold to authors, and they ensure that more business owners like you can benefit from the information provided. Below, I've provided the link to leave a review: <u>Give a 5-star Review for Before You Sign That Lease</u>....

BIO

Raphael Collazo is a licensed commercial real estate agent specializing in retail, industrial, office and income producing properties. Transitioning from a career in software, Raphael brings a strong technical background and a love for dissecting complex problems to his client interactions. These characteristics enable him to provide innovative and effective real estate solutions to help his clients get the most out of each transaction. As a real estate investor himself, Raphael is acutely aware of what investors look for when evaluating commercial property. As a result, he's able to offer a unique perspective and help his clients make the best possible decision based on their business and financial goals.

Prior to joining the Grisanti Group, Raphael worked as a software implementation consultant for FAST Enterprises, a software company that provides C.O.T.S software products to government agencies. Having lived and worked in various locations around the United States and abroad including Pordenone, Italy, Phoenix, Arizona, Washington D.C, San Juan, Puerto Rico and Louisville Kentucky, Raphael has gained a unique understanding of cultural intricacies and has leveraged those experiences to expand his professional network to better serve his clients.

Along with being a full-time commercial real estate agent, Raphael is also the author of the Millennial Playbook series, a book series that focuses on personal and professional development topics for young professionals. As a performance coach and speaker, he's also had the opportunity to speak to thousands of students and professionals on a wide range of subjects. Raphael graduated from Arizona State University in 2013 with a bachelor's degree in industrial engineering and a minor in economics.

BOOK RECOMMENDATIONS

Although this book is a comprehensive guide to leasing commercial real estate, it's most certainly not the only one that offers valuable insights to business owners. For that reason, I've dedicated this section to highlighting other outstanding books that will help you along your entrepreneurial journey. If you would like to recommend any business/entrepreneurship books, feel free to reach out! I'm always looking for great reads to expand my knowledge.

Negotiating Commercial Real Estate Leases – Martin I. Zankel

Although this reads like a law journal at times, it's by far the most comprehensive book I have read on the subject of commercial lease agreements. Martin Zankel, Emeritus Counsel at *"Bartko Zankel & Bunzel"*, has been practicing real estate law for over 40 years and has worked with some of the largest corporations on the planet to help them effectively navigate the commercial real estate landscape.

Throughout the book, Martin does a great job walking through a seemingly endless supply of contract provisions and verbiage that you should consider as you negotiate your commercial lease agreement. If you're currently working with a commercial real estate agent, share this book with them so they are properly informed and in position to negotiate the best commercial real estate lease on your behalf. If you're interested in purchasing the book, I've provided the link here: https://amzn.to/3gLD7wg

The Due-Diligence Handbook for Commercial Real Estate – Brian Hennessey

Although this book was primarily written for those looking to purchase commercial real estate, the concepts discussed also apply to business owners interested in leasing commercial property. With over 35 years of experience in the commercial real estate space, Brian has managed every aspect of the real estate transaction: from developing acquisition and disposition strategies; to conducting market and feasibility analyses; negotiating and executing leases and multi-state portfolio transactions totaling approximately 12 million square feet at values in excess of $2 billion. Given his vast experience, he has a wealth of knowledge to draw upon.

Since writing this book back in 2012, he has made a name for himself teaching others how to properly perform due diligence on commercial property. As a business owner, it's your job to inspect the mechanicals, structure, roof and other building components prior to taking possession of your space. With this book as your guide, you can mitigate the risk of major building components failing throughout your tenancy. If you're interested in purchasing the book, I've provided the link here: https://amzn.to/3a2S6jd

80/20 Sales and Marketing – Perry Marshall

This is probably one of the best sales and marketing books that I've read; bar none. The premise revolves around the idea that *"20% of all your actions, account for 80% of your results"*. Because of this, if you're able to isolate the activities that give you out-sized returns in the least amount of work hours, you can amplify your results over time. This book was a real eye opener for me because it forced me to scrutinize the actions I took each day to grow my business. Once I took the time to do this, I adjusted my approach and have since been able to achieve much more favorable results in my business. If you're interested in purchasing the book, I've provided the link here: https://amzn.to/31o7lPO

The E-Myth Revisited – Michael E. Gerber

Like the 80/20 Rule, this book fostered a paradigm shift for me. As a small business owner, I'm often forced to wear many hats within the organization. Not only am I the CEO of my company, I'm also the CIO, CMO, CFO and every other executive position you can think of. However, if I hope to scale my business one day, I need to work more *"on"* my business rather than of *"in"* it.

If you want to eventually enjoy the fruits of your labor, you must set aside time each week to perform various activities such as building marketing systems, hiring/training an employee, developing a procedure manual that you will issue to your entire staff etc. These activities and many others like them are ones that will have a lasting impact on the longevity of your business. If you're interested in purchasing the book, I've provided the link below: https://amzn.to/33zXAAu

Profit-First - Mike Micalowicz

Lucky for you, I saved the best business book for last. Mike Micalowicz has been through it all. He founded, grew and sold a successful IT company in his 20's only to nearly go bankrupt shortly thereafter. After seeing the err in his ways, he resolved to create more sustainable and profitable businesses that positively impact the world. Over the course of his 20+ year career, he's helped thousands of entrepreneurs improve their businesses by optimizing their operations and shifting their strategy away from *"growing at all costs"* to *"being profitable from day one"*. This book was a game changer for me because it allowed me to organize my business finances in such a way that promoted profitability from the get-go. If you're interested in purchasing his book, I've provided the link here: https://amzn.to/2F2sveH

REAL ESTATE TERMINOLOGY

To properly digest the content of this book, it's important to understand the terminology that is regularly used in the commercial real estate industry. For that reason, I decided to dedicate this section of the book to highlighting some of the most common commercial real estate terms, phrases, and expressions. By learning these, you'll have the proper framework to assess the merits of a commercial property and maximize the value you receive from the transaction.

> **Disclaimer:** Depending on the context, some of these terms may have more than one definition. Because this book discusses leasing commercial real estate, this is the lens I used when describing the terms.

Add on Factor: The percentage of a building's gross usable space that is added to each tenant's rented space to determine their total rent.

Adjusted Basis: The original cost or other basis of a property, minus the depreciation deductions and increased by capital expenditures. For example, let's imagine that someone buys a lot for $100,000. They then build a retail facility on it for $600,000. Finally, they depreciate the improvements for tax purposes at the rate of $15,000 per year. After three years, the adjusted basis of the property would be $655,000 [$100,000 + $600,000 - (3 x $15,000)].

Amortization: The paying off of debt over time in equal installments.

Assessment: The determined value of a property for tax purposes. A property's assessed value is multiplied by the local and state tax rates to determine the total property taxes to be paid each year.

Balloon Payment: A lump sum paid at the end of a loan's term that is significantly larger than all the payments made before it.

Base Rent: The minimum rent due each month to occupy a commercial space. The base rent does not include expenses such as property taxes, insurance, building maintenance etc.

Build Out: The work that will need to be done to make the property ready for its intended use.

Breakpoint: The point where by the tenant begins paying additional rent in a percentage lease agreement. This metric is calculated by taking the base monthly rent and dividing it by the percentage rate. For example, if a tenant signs a percentage lease with a base rent of $5,000 and a percentage rent of 7%, the sales volume breakpoint would be $71,428 per month ($5000/0.07).

Common Area Maintenance (C.A.M): The net charges billed to tenants in a commercial triple-net (NNN) lease to maintain the common areas of a commercial property. These areas may include shared hallways, bathrooms, parking lots, elevators etc.

Common Area Maintenance Cap (C.A.M Cap): The maximum amount of C.A.M. expenses a tenant is responsible for paying in a given timeframe.

Capital Gain: The profit that results from the sale of an asset. In commercial real estate, it's the difference between the amount you paid for the property and the price you eventually sell it for.

Capitalization Rate (Cap Rate): A real estate valuation measure used to compare different real estate investments. It's calculated by taking the net operating income (N.O.I) of a property and dividing it by the property value. For example, if a property produces $75,000 in N.O.I and it's listed for sale at $1,000,000, the cap rate of the property is 7.5%.

Cash Flow: The amount of cash and cash equivalents (i.e. commercial paper, treasury bills, short term government bonds, marketable securities, money market holdings etc.) being transferred into and out of a business.

Cash-on Cash Return: A rate of return often used in real estate transactions that calculates the cash income earned on the cash invested in the property. For example, if a property produced $12,000 per year after covering operating expenses and the mortgage and your initial investment in the deal was $120,000, your cash on cash return would be 10% ($12,000/$120,000).

Commercial Real Estate: Buildings or land intended to generate a profit, either from business use, capital gain or rental income. Examples of commercial real estate include multifamily, office, hospitality, industrial, raw land and retail.

Common Area: Those areas that are available for common use by all tenants, groups of tenants and their invitees. In other words, it defines the *"area which is available for use by more than one person"*.

Class: A term used to define the quality of a piece of real estate. Class A properties are the newest, best located and most sought-after in a particular market while Class C properties are generally older, marginally located and in need of maintenance.

Cost of Occupancy: The costs associated with occupying a space in a commercial building. These costs may include rent, real estate taxes, personal property taxes, building insurance, etc.

Co-Tenancy: A situation whereby more than one tenant is occupying a commercial building. This is most common in multi-tenant properties such as strip-centers, office buildings, industrial complexes etc.

Doing Business As (D.B.A): A business name used by companies that don't want to operate under their registered legal name.

Demographics: Statistical data relating to the population and particular groups within it.

Depreciation: A reduction in the value of an asset with the passage of time, due to normal wear and tear.

Due Diligence: An in-depth investigation of property to confirm facts related to its acquisition. During the due diligence period, you should review financial documents, service contracts, conduct tenant interviews as well as a host of other materials.

Effective Rent: The remaining cash a landlord receives after paying all expenses for operating the property. For example, if a tenant leases a space for $3,000 per month and the landlord is responsible for covering operating expenses of $1,000 per month, their effective rent for the space would be $2,000 per month.

Environmental Hazards: Something that has the potential to threaten the surrounding natural environment and/or affect people's health. In commercial real estate, the most common environmental hazards include underground gas tanks, dry cleaning chemicals, toxic waste, sewage run-off etc.

Exclusivity: Allows a tenant to use the premises for a specific use (i.e. restaurant, men's apparel, nail salon etc.) and restricts other tenants from pursuing a similar use.

Expense Stop: A dollar value for operating expenses above which a tenant is responsible for covering the remaining balance. For example, if the landlord is responsible for paying all operating expenses up to $500 per month, any expenses above that amount will become the responsibility of the tenant.

Feasibility Analysis: An investigation whose purpose is to determine the viability of purchasing a commercial property.

Fixed Costs: Expenses that are constant, regardless of the quantity. Examples of fixed costs include rent, real estate taxes and insurance.

Flex Space: Used to describe a combination of light industrial and office space.

Foundation: The support that a building rests on. These usually consist of slab, crawlspace, or basement foundations.

Free Rent: A period where rent payments are not collected. Generally, it's an incentive landlords offer financially strong tenants to encourage them to sign a long-term lease in their commercial space.

Full-Service Gross (FSG) Lease: A lease whereby the tenant pays a base rent and the landlord covers all operating expenses related to the tenant's occupancy such as common area maintenance, utilities, property insurance, and property taxes.

Gap Analysis: The difference between supply and demand of commercial real estate. This value is calculated by subtracting the tenant demand for space (measured in SF) by the amount of available SF of space in the market. A negative number signifies oversaturation while a positive number represents excess demand.

Gross Area: The total area within the walls of a building structure, including the walls themselves and *"unlivable"* space.

Gross Lease: A commercial lease where the tenant is responsible for paying a flat rental amount while the landlord is responsible for paying costs associated with property ownership including, but not limited to, taxes, utilities, water etc.

Gross Rent Multiplier (GRM): A ratio of the price of a real estate investment compared to its annual rental income before expenses. Investors use the GRM to determine the number of years it would take for a property to pay for itself based on its yearly gross rent.

Ground Lease: An agreement in which a tenant is permitted to develop a piece of property on the land they are renting.

Heating, Ventilation, and Air Conditioning (HVAC): A term used to describe the equipment used to keep buildings at a comfortable temperature.

Highest and Best Use: The optimal use for the property and/or space. For example, the highest and best use for a building in a high traffic area that has a grease trap, commercial kitchen hood and a drive thru is likely a restaurant.

Hold Over Fees – Fees charged to a tenant if they remain on site after their lease expiration date. Generally, these fees are added on to your base rent and range anywhere between 25-100% of your monthly rent.

Hold Over Tenant: A tenant who remains on the premises after the expiration date of the lease. If this occurs, hold-over fees are generally assess on top of their base rent payments.

Kick Out Clause: A clause that allows the tenant and/or landlord to cancel the lease after a pre-determined period and/or if certain conditions have not been met.

Lease: A legally binding document detailing the terms of a real estate agreement.

Lease Buyout: A clause that allows the tenant or landlord to break the lease by paying a pre-determined amount. Generally, this amount is equivalent to several months in rent.

Lessee: An individual or corporation who has the right to use the space outlined in their lease agreement. Also known as the *"tenant"*.

Lessor: An individual or corporation who leases property to another. Also known as the *"landlord"*.

Letter of Intent (LOI): A document that declares a preliminary commitment of one party to do business with another based on an agreement of a particular set of terms. This is a non-binding document.

Load Factor: The percentage of space on a floor or building that is not usable. This ratio is expressed by taking the rentable area divided by usable area minus one.

Market Analysis: The activity of gathering information about conditions that affect a marketplace. Used to assess the suitability of a location for a given purpose.

Market Rates: The rent a commercial space, without rent or income restrictions, would command in the open market considering its location, features, and amenities.

Market Value: The most probable price a property can be sold for in a given market.

Metropolitan Statistical Area (MSA): An area containing a substantial population nucleus, together with adjacent communities having a high degree of economic and social integration. In other words, it's the area in and around a city or town.

Moving Allowance: A pre-determined amount a landlord or owner will pay to cover a tenant's moving expenses.

Net lease: A lease in which the tenant pays all operating expenses in addition to rent (i.e. taxes, insurance, maintenance.)

Net Operating Income: A calculation used to describe as well as its potential value. A property's NOI is calculated by taking its revenue and subtracting a market vacancy rate as well as other reasonably necessary operating expenses.

Occupancy Cost: The costs associated with occupying a space. These expenses include, but are not limited to, rent, real estate taxes, personal property taxes, insurance on building contents etc.

Operating Expenses: The expenses associated with keeping a building operational. These expenses include, but are not limited to, utilities, water, cleaning, accounting, capital expenditures, repairs and maintenance etc.

Option: A clause within a lease agreement that allows a tenant to renew their lease for a set period based on pre-determined terms.

Pass-Through Lease: A contract where specified operating expenses *"pass through"* from the landlord to the tenant. These additional expenses can include any combination of property taxes, insurance, maintenance, repairs and utilities.

Percentage Lease: A lease that requires a tenant to pay a base rent plus a percentage of monthly sales volume above a *"breakpoint"*.

Potential Rental Income: The amount of rent a property could generate if it was fully occupied and leased at market rates.

Property Type: The classification of commercial real estate based on its primary use. Commercial property types include multifamily, office, industrial, retail, hospitality and land.

Rate of Return: The net gain or loss of an investment over a specified time period. This metric is expressed as a percentage of your initial investment.

Real Estate Cycles: A sequence of recurrent events reflected in demographic, economic and emotional factors that affect supply and demand for property. These cycles either have a negative or positive impact on the property markets.

Rent Concessions: A period of free or reduced rent afforded to the tenant by the landlord.

Rent Escalators: Language within a commercial lease agreement whereby operating expenses, base rent, and/or taxes may increase at pre-determined times. These increases are either monetary intervals (i.e. $50, $100, $150 etc.) or percentage intervals (i.e. 2%, 3%, 4% etc.)

Replacement Cost: The amount it would take to replace a property at the present time.

Second Generation Space: A property that was occupied by a previous tenant and was built out for their use.

Site Analysis: A process used to assess the feasibility of a property for a given use based on characteristics including, but not limited to, zoning, traffic counts, demographics, nearby suppliers etc.

Site Selection: A process used to identify the best site given a desired use.

Square Feet: A unit of measurement in commercial real estate used to describe the floor area of a space. For example, if a space were 50 feet wide and 50 ft deep, the square footage of the space would equal 2,500 SF (50 ft x 50 ft).

Sublease: The leasing of a property to a subtenant by the existing tenant. This event occurs when a tenant would like to get out of their existing lease but is unable to break the lease outright. If a *"sublease"* clause is included in the lease agreement, the tenant has the right to lease the space to another tenant barring the landlord's approval.

Tenant: An individual or business that occupies land or property owned by a landlord.

Tenant Improvement Allowance (T.I.A): The amount a landlord is willing to spend on renovating a space to fit the use of a new tenant. This metric is usually expressed on a per square foot basis.

Triple-net lease: A lease agreement whereby the tenant is responsible for paying all property expenses including real estate taxes, building insurance, and maintenance.

Turnkey: A fully renovated property that a tenant can move into without making any modifications.

Useable Square Feet: The total square feet of an area that is unique to the tenant and is not accessible to other tenants on the premises.

Variable Expenses: Costs that change over time. In commercial real estate, these expenses may include utilities, water, trash removal, cleaning, repairs, maintenance etc.

Zoning: Municipal or local laws or regulations that dictate how a piece of real estate can and cannot be used in certain geographic areas. This designation will determine if a property is considered commercial, residential etc.

REFERENCES

"Demographics of Social Media Users and Adoption in the United States." Pew Research Center: Internet, Science & Tech, Pew Research Center, 5 June 2020, www.pewresearch.org/internet/fact-sheet/social-media/

"37% Of Shoppers Use Social Media to Influence Their Purchases-Transaction: An ECommerce Agency." Transaction, 2018, transaction.agency/ecommerce-statistics/37-of-shoppers- use-social-media-to-influence-their-purchases/.

Murphy, Rosie. "Local Consumer Review Survey: How Customers Use Online Reviews." BrightLocal, 9 July 2020, www.brightlocal.com/research/local-consumer-review-survey/?SSAID=314743&SSCID=71k4_mv2pj.

"Local SEO Ranking Factors Study." Local SEO Guide, 23 Dec. 2019, www.localseoguide.com/guides/local-seo-ranking-factors/.

"About Us." BNI, 6 July 2020, www.bni.com/about.

Flint, Michael, et al. *"Cash Flow: The Reason 82% of Small Businesses Fail."* Preferred CFO, 30 July 2020, www.preferredcfo.com/cash-flow-reason-small-businesses-fail/#:~:text= We know that the majority,failure of a small business.

Made in the USA
Monee, IL
28 December 2022

23968496R00075